FINANCING THE OCEAN BACK TO HEALTH IN SOUTHEAST ASIA

APPROACHES FOR MAINSTREAMING BLUE FINANCE

DECEMBER 2021

ACGF
ASEAN CATALYTIC GREEN FINANCE FACILITY

ADB

Contents

Tables, Figures, and Boxes

Foreword

The United Nations and the global community recognize the importance of ocean health through the Sustainable Development Goal (SDG) 14: Life Below Water, which focuses on the inclusion of conservation and sustainable use of the ocean. Despite the environmental and economic benefits of healthy oceans, a growing number of natural and human-induced threats to this precious resource continues unabated. Eight million tons of plastic are entering the ocean every year and mostly from Asia and the Pacific, along with huge volumes of agricultural pollutants and untreated wastewater. Climate change is causing rising sea levels, ocean warming, and acidification, while unsustainable fishing is depleting fish stocks. Not taking action means the death of 90% of coral reefs by 2052 and the loss of all commercially exploitable wild fish stocks by 2048. With an estimated 1 billion people dependent on seafood and a global fishing market worth an annual $100 billion, this would seriously affect the global economy.

Recognition of the growing threats to the ocean has resulted in an increase in global "blue" initiatives. The ocean's contribution to the global economy is estimated at $2.5 trillion, and this "blue economy" is defined as the sustainable use of ocean and coastal resources to drive economic growth and improve livelihoods, while protecting and nurturing marine ecosystems. There are increasing opportunities in sustainable tourism, food production, wastewater treatment, integrated solid waste management, and sustainable coastal infrastructure, but securing these opportunities requires large investments, and governments and donors cannot meet the needs alone. This shortage of funds, estimated by ADB at $459 billion annually, can only be met by a significant ramp-up in flows from commercial and institutional finance, capital markets, and public-private partnerships. Traditional blended finance vehicles play a crucial role in increasing blue economy investments from nonsovereign sources, but more innovative structures like blue bonds, debt-for-nature swaps, credit enhancements, SDG bonds, and other innovative approaches to tapping the region's capital markets should be explored to suit the needs of specific projects.

To accelerate the investments in the blue economy, ADB is currently implementing its Action Plan for Healthy Oceans and Sustainable Blue Economies, which targets to expand financing and technical assistance for ocean health and marine economy projects to $5 billion from 2019 to 2024, including cofinancing from partners. It will focus on four areas: creating inclusive livelihoods and business opportunities in sustainable tourism and fisheries; protecting and restoring coastal and marine ecosystems and key rivers; reducing land-based sources of marine pollution, including plastics, wastewater, and agricultural runoff; and improving sustainability in port and coastal infrastructure development. The Southeast Asia Department (SERD) of ADB is piloting ADB's Oceans Financing Initiative to help address these challenges and boost investment in the region, with support from the Association of Southeast Asian Nations (ASEAN) Catalytic Green Finance Facility (ACGF) (under the ASEAN Infrastructure Fund), the Republic of Korea, and World Wide Fund for Nature. This will help protect and restore marine ecosystems and secure the growth of marine economies in the region.

In this context, SERD and the ACGF have developed this paper to provide an overview of the blue economy with a particular focus on the investment approaches, opportunities, and finance mechanisms that are available to promote and catalyze funds for a sustainable ocean economy (i.e., multilateral/bilateral sources, a market-based approach, incentives, regulations, etc.). This report proposes a blue finance mechanism which can provide tailored concessional finance and de-risking instruments to blue economy projects along with support for structuring sustainable project models and improving institutional capacity. It also looks at the need to align those with a cohesive development framework for the blue economy.

ADB will continue to play a key role in supporting ASEAN countries to develop sustainable and bankable infrastructure projects that will stimulate the blue economy, while supporting SDG 14: Life Below Water and the targets of the Paris Agreement.

We must restore and protect our oceans now to secure the future of Asia and the Pacific, because when oceans thrive, people thrive.

Ramesh Subramaniam
Director General, Southeast Asia Department
Asian Development Bank

Key Messages from Peer Reviewers

Norimasa Shimomura, resident representative in Indonesia, United Nations Development Programme. Ocean is the lifeline of humanity. Its rich biodiversity provides abundant benefits to the sustenance of societies and environment worldwide. Nonetheless, the rate and scale of our economic activity could risk massive degradation—at an unprecedented scale. Therefore, we must rethink our approach in managing our oceans and seas into a sustainable economic model that could guarantee their existence for future generations. A collaborative action to leverage innovative financing for a sustainable blue ecosystem is urgently needed. The United Nations Development Programme (UNDP) is pleased to be working with the Asian Development Bank (ADB) in this area, through a forthcoming joint Blue Finance Accelerator platform in Indonesia. This initiative will be particularly useful in boosting the local blue economy and attract global flows of capital after the coronavirus disease (COVID-19) pandemic. Blue financing instruments, such as ocean impact funds, blended finance and blue bonds can protect the oceans from detrimental activities and attract sustainable investments for long-term ecological and social benefits. Our partnership with ADB is in line with UNDP's core mission to promote environmental sustainability for a lasting and inclusive prosperity, as heralded by the 2030 Agenda for Sustainable Development. Our sincere congratulation to ADB for formulating this rich report which serves as a reminder of our much-needed collective responsibility; for the public and private sectors to partner and create a healthy blue economy.

Seth Tan, executive director, Infrastructure Asia. This work by ADB is very timely as it highlights the challenges in the blue sector and the opportunities in blue finance. The territorial waters of Southeast Asia comprise an area three times the land area, and issues like river pollution, river plastics, are now affecting livelihoods and economic development. As a regional infrastructure facilitation office under the Government of Singapore, Infrastructure Asia is pleased to work with ADB and the ASEAN Catalytic Green Finance Facility to help raise the awareness of the solutions available to catalyze further sustainable blue economy infrastructure and blue finance. This report could be very useful to inspire governments to create more enabling environments to attract more international private sector into their country's sustainable blue infrastructure.

Melissa Wright, Vibrant Oceans Initiative lead at Bloomberg Philanthropies. The blue economy relies on a healthy and thriving ocean, which in turn relies on access to sustainable finance for ocean infrastructure projects. This ADB new report shows that to bridge the funding gap and ensure coastal communities across Asia continue to benefit from the blue economy, we must double down on innovative finance strategies and cross-sector partnerships. Bloomberg Philanthropies and the Vibrant Oceans Initiative look forward to continuing to pursue collaborative opportunities to combat climate change and ensure a healthy, sustainable ocean and planet for generations to come.

Bruce Dunn, chief, Safeguards, Sustainable Development and Climate Change Department, Asian Development Bank. The oceans are the economic heartbeat of Southeast Asia. Blue economy sectors such as tourism, fisheries, and aquaculture are major contributors to the region's economies, fish supply, as well as household and local food security. However, climate change, pollution, illegal and unregulated fishing, and unsustainable development have pushed our oceans to the brink of collapse. As governments shift their focus to respond and recover from the coronavirus disease pandemic, the pressure on these fragile ocean ecosystems has increased due to a surge in plastic consumption, weakened enforcement of illegal fishing practices, and less available funding to sustainably manage ocean resources. This report is a timely reminder on the growing need for sustainable blue economies and innovative ocean finance mechanisms. A huge opportunity exists to use blended finance, credit enhancements, and smart financial structures to decrease the ocean funding gap and scale up ocean investments to meet the challenge at hand. ADB, through the Action Plan for Healthy Oceans and Sustainable Blue Economies, is committed to growing ocean investments by providing strategic and sustainable support to Asia and the Pacific, so that economies and businesses are future fit, able to thrive in the long run, and are resilient to identified future risks and stressors. Protecting the ocean reduces poverty and saves lives, and we must all work together to create impact at scale.

About the Authors

This document was prepared by an Asian Development Bank (ADB) team led by Anouj Mehta, unit head, Green and Innovative Finance and the ASEAN Catalytic Green Finance Facility (ACGF). The team included ACGF consultants Raghu Dharmapuri Tirumala and Marina Lopez Andrich, working within the Innovation Hub in ADB's Southeast Asia Department. Ramesh Subramaniam, director general, Southeast Asia Department, provided overall supervision in the preparation of this document, which also benefited from significant peer reviewer inputs and feedback.

The team benefited from the essential collaboration with the ADB Environment Thematic Group of the Sustainable Development and Climate Change Department (SDCC) and Bruce Dunn, chief of Safeguards, with guidance from Deborah Robertson, environment specialist, and special inputs from Melissa Walsh, SDCC consultant and program manager for the Ocean Finance Initiative.

Acknowledgments

The lead team of authors for this paper acknowledges the contributions made from members of the Asian Development Bank (ADB) Southeast Asia Innovation Hub and Association of Southeast Asian Nations Catalytic Green Finance Facility (ACGF) teams, including Joven Balbosa (advisor), Alfredo Perdiguero (director), Raquel Tabanao (associate knowledge management officer), Ma. Luisa Victoria Cadiz-Andrion (consultant, ACGF), and Vinh Prag (consultant, ACGF). Editing by Layla Amar. Design and layout by Edith Creus.

The team also thanks specially the valuable inputs from Ingrid Van Wees, ADB Vice-President for Finance and Risk Management, Bruce Dunn, chief of Safeguards of the ADB Sustainable Development and Climate Change Department (SDCC), and the ADB Environment Thematic Group of SDCC, with guidance from Deborah Robertson, environment specialist, and special inputs from Melissa Walsh, SDCC consultant and program manager for the Ocean Finance Initiative.

Overall supervision was provided by Ramesh Subramaniam, director general, ADB Southeast Asia Department.

The team greatly benefited from the guidance and inputs provided by the following peer reviewers during conceptualization as well as the final draft stage of the publication.

Peer Reviewers and Advisors

- Norimasa Shimomura, resident representative in Indonesia, United Nations Development Programme
- Seth Tan, executive director, Infrastructure Asia
- Melissa Wright, Vibrant Oceans Initiative lead at Bloomberg Philanthropies
- Nicolas Pascal, executive director and co-founder, Blue Finance
- Rob Kaplan, founder and chief executive officer, Circulate Capital
- Chris Gorell Barnes, founding partner, Ocean 14 Capital
- Max Gottschalk, founding partner, Ocean 14 Capital
- Michael C. Huang, research fellow, Ocean Policy Research Institute of the Sasakawa Peace Foundation
- Kristian Teleki, director, Sustainable Ocean Initiative, World Resources Institute
- Ben Hart, research associate, Sustainable Ocean Initiative, World Resources Institute
- Ingrid Van Wees, Vice-President, Finance and Risk Management, ADB
- Bruce Dunn, chief, Safeguards, Sustainable Development and Climate Change Department, ADB
- Deborah Robertson, environment specialist, Environment Thematic Group, Sustainable Development and Climate Change Department, ADB
- Melissa Walsh, blue finance consultant, Environment Thematic Group, Sustainable Development and Climate Change Department, ADB

Abbreviations

ACGF	ASEAN Catalytic Green Finance Facility
ADB	Asian Development Bank
ASEAN	Association of Southeast Asian Nations
BRI	Belt and Road Initiative (People's Republic of China)
CBI	Climate Bonds Initiative
CSR	corporate social responsibility
DMC	developing member country
EIB	European Investment Bank
EU	European Union
GDP	gross domestic product
GEF	Global Environment Facility
IBRD	International Bank for Reconstruction and Development
MDB	multilateral development bank
MPA	marine protected area
OECD	Organisation for Economic Co-operation and Development
PEMSEA	Partnerships in Environmental Management for the Seas of East Asia
PPP	public–private partnership
SDCC	Sustainable Development and Climate Change Department
SDG	Sustainable Development Goal
SERD	Southeast Asia Department
SIDS	small island developing state
SOC	State of Ocean and Coasts
SWM	solid waste management

tpd	tonnes per day
UNCTAD	United Nations Conference on Trade and Development
UNDP	United Nations Development Programme
UNEP	United Nations Environment Programme
UNFCCC	United Nations Framework Convention on Climate Change
USAID	United States Agency for International Development

Executive Summary

The ocean's contribution to the economy has been described as the "blue economy," the sustainable use of ocean and coastal resources to drive economic growth and improve livelihoods, while protecting and nurturing healthy marine ecosystems. The importance of ocean health is recognized by the Sustainable Development Goals (SDG) through SDG 14: Life Below Water, which is focused on the inclusion of conservation and sustainable use of the ocean. Despite the environmental and economic benefits, a growing number of natural and human-induced threats to this precious resource continues unabated. Climate change, environmental pollution, unsustainable fishing and mining practices, unregulated coastal development, and dumping of solid and liquid wastes pose a grave threat to marine life and humanity, undermining the productivity of our ocean. Recognition of the growing threats to the ocean have resulted in an increase in global "blue" initiatives.

Given the wealth and biodiversity of its natural resources, the potential for a vibrant blue economy is especially high in Southeast Asia, where intensive farming and aquaculture, rapid urbanization and industrialization, and the rising prevalence of plastic pollution are damaging the region's waters. Economies of the Association of Southeast Asian Nations have launched initiatives to stimulate a sustainable blue economy, mostly financed by public sector spending and assisted in part by international organizations.

The ocean, if treated like a country, is the seventh-largest economy in the world with an estimated value of $2.5 trillion. However, financing remains a key concern for realizing the blue economy potential. The nature and characteristics of blue economy projects imply that financing options need to extend far beyond the conventional multilateral and bilateral aid to leveraging blended finance options and attracting a diverse set of impact investors. Blended finance vehicles have a role to play in increasing blue economy investments, but more innovative structures like blue bonds, debt-for-nature swaps, credit enhancements, and social impact bonds to tap regional capital markets could be explored to suit the needs of specific projects.

A key challenge encountered by blue finance is the lack of clear definitions and project selection criteria. In the absence of well-defined principles and a framework for "blue economy investing," investors will shy away from this sector. Standardization in terms of transparency, independent verification, and reporting is critical for building investors' confidence in environmental credentials and performance of the investments. Blue finance principles are being developed by many agencies including the Asian Development Bank (ADB), the United Nations Environment Programme, and partners that seek to align the project outcomes to blue economy impacts, and these frameworks are expected to provide a template for investing in the blue economy.

To accelerate the investments in the blue economy, this report proposes an ocean health mechanism, structured as a facility which can provide tailored concessional finance and de-risking instruments to blue economy projects along with support for structuring sustainable project models and improving institutional capacity.

A blue finance investment facility with provisions for technical assistance could be set up either at a regional or national level, to identify, originate, design, and structure projects based on ocean finance frameworks and standards, along with an objective to achieve desired financial bankability metrics. The capital structure of such a facility could be a mixture of grant funds, zero interest loans, and concessional funds. The facility could draw its funds from a combination of government budgetary allocations (including those committed in climate change nationally determined contributions), multilateral, bilateral agencies and development partners, private, philanthropic, institutional, and commercial capital.

The funds could be used to support (i) specific government-originated projects including public–private partnership projects (through an integrated package comprising project development, structuring, and financing components using a variety of investment instruments) that have limited revenue streams but have considerable potential for avoided costs and environmental savings; (ii) individual projects promoted by private investors that adhere to the blue principles; and (iii) knowledge, awareness, and capacity building for stakeholders and institutions concerned and pipeline creation.

It is expected that a significant component of the blue finance mechanism would be to catalyze high-impact projects, which the public sector project proponents will be mandated to develop and implement. The capacity-building support could be in the form of assistance in generating and developing project pipelines, preliminary project structuring, monitoring, measurement and impact assessment, institutional strengthening of project sponsors, policy, governance and institutional strengthening, and knowledge dissemination. The instruments that could potentially be part of the mechanism include concessional finance, guarantee for bonds and revenue support structures, and subscription to first loss tranches.

The blue finance mechanism could assist the proponents in developing innovative finance instruments. One such instruments could be an "ocean health credit." This ocean health credit could be configured either as a certificate or structured note or as predetermined payments to the project for achieving desired impacts.

The impact investors and project stakeholders could issue ocean health credits, an instrument that offers a rate of return comparable with other similar environmental, social, and governance (ESG) products, when held to maturity. The returns on the ocean health credit could be structured with minimal payments in the initial years (to provide immediate low-cost funds to the project proponents), with rates stepping up over a period. The investors could have the option to either hold on until maturity and exit (with returns similar to other ESG instruments) or can be given an option to exchange their ocean health credits into equity. The conversion into equity would provide these investors a stake in the project and increased community participation. The guarantee component of the blue finance framework would be extended to the full principal and interest for the ocean health credit investors at the time of exit. The direct and indirect benefits or "avoided costs" (relating to health care, livelihoods, education, credit, infrastructure, political participation, etc.) resulting from blue economy interventions could be captured and financially valued, which could potentially become an additionality to the project revenues.

An alternate structure of an ocean health credit could entail the national entity or sovereign (through the blue finance mechanism) providing a predetermined annual payment or ocean health credits to a project's implementing entity, linked to performance or impact indicators that a project needs to achieve, such as those set out in the ADB Ocean Finance Framework. The functioning of ocean health credits should be seen as aligned with the principle of "avoided costs" from alleviating future economic or health disasters, such as diseases arising from lack of access to clean water, polluted river bodies, or decline in fishing stocks. An estimate of such avoided costs could provide a benchmark to limit the level of ocean health credits provided to a project.

The blue finance mechanism could support blue economy projects initiated by private sponsors, which have untested revenue streams, or those adopting new technologies, or those with significant blue economy benefits. The facility could offer a guarantee ("ocean health credit guarantee") at concessional rates on debt repayment to the blue bond holders for a defined percentage of the principal and interest payments. Appropriate market sounding and context-based structuring need to be undertaken prior to the launch of the ocean health credit mechanism.

1 THE BLUE ECONOMY IN CRISIS

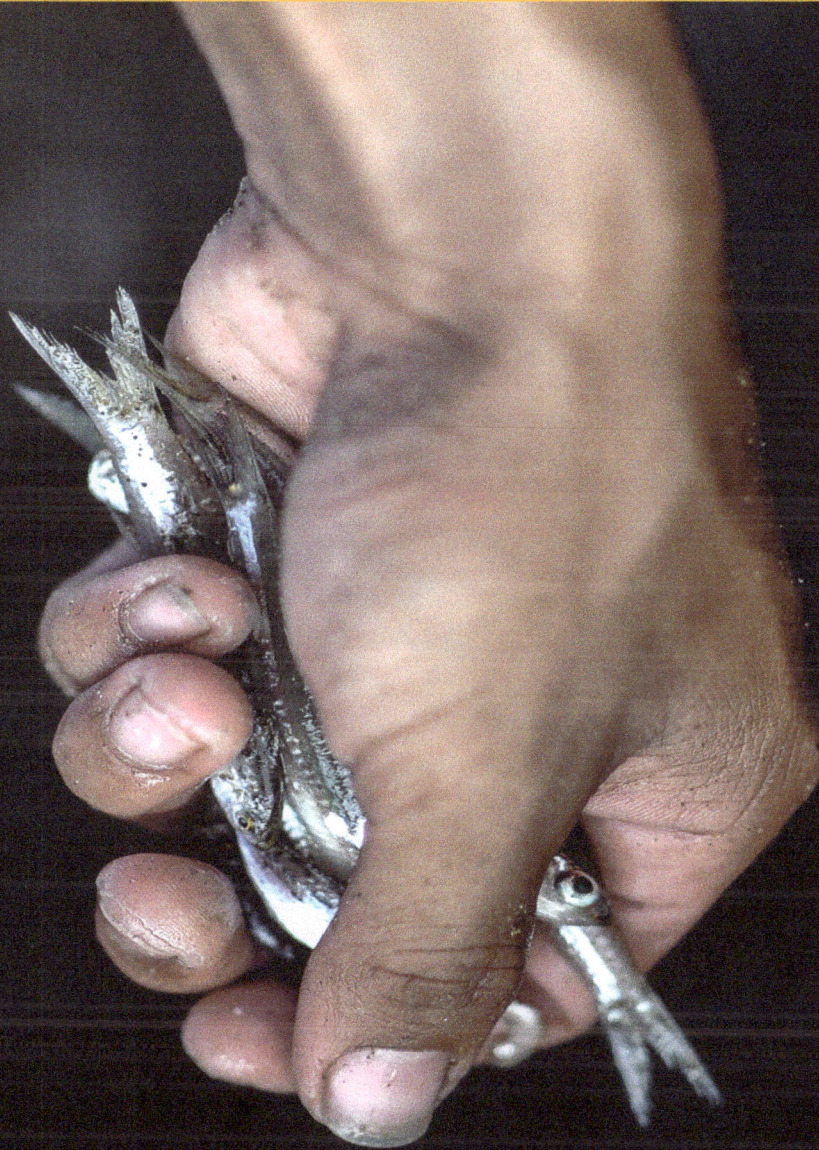

A handful of fish. A fisherman unloads buckets of fish from a boat in Makassar, South Sulawesi, Indonesia (photo by Eric Sales/ADB).

"Now, as never before, we have the chance to save what's left of the living systems that support life on our planet. We should act as if our lives depend on a healthy ocean—because they do."

SYLVIA EARLE, FOUNDER, MISSION BLUE

A. The Blue Economy: An Overview

The ocean regulates climate; drives weather patterns that determine rainfall, droughts, and floods; sustains a rich diversity of species; and provides nourishment to billions of people through seafood (Figure 1). It also provides employment to millions of people in biotechnology, energy, fishing, shipping, tourism, and other sectors. The market value of coastal and marine resources and related industries is an estimated $3 trillion to $5 trillion, which is nearly 5% of global gross domestic product (GDP).[1] In some East Asian countries, the ocean economy accounts for 15%–20% of GDP.[2]

> *It has been estimated that 50%-80% of the oxygen we breathe comes from our ocean.*
>
> **National Ocean Service**

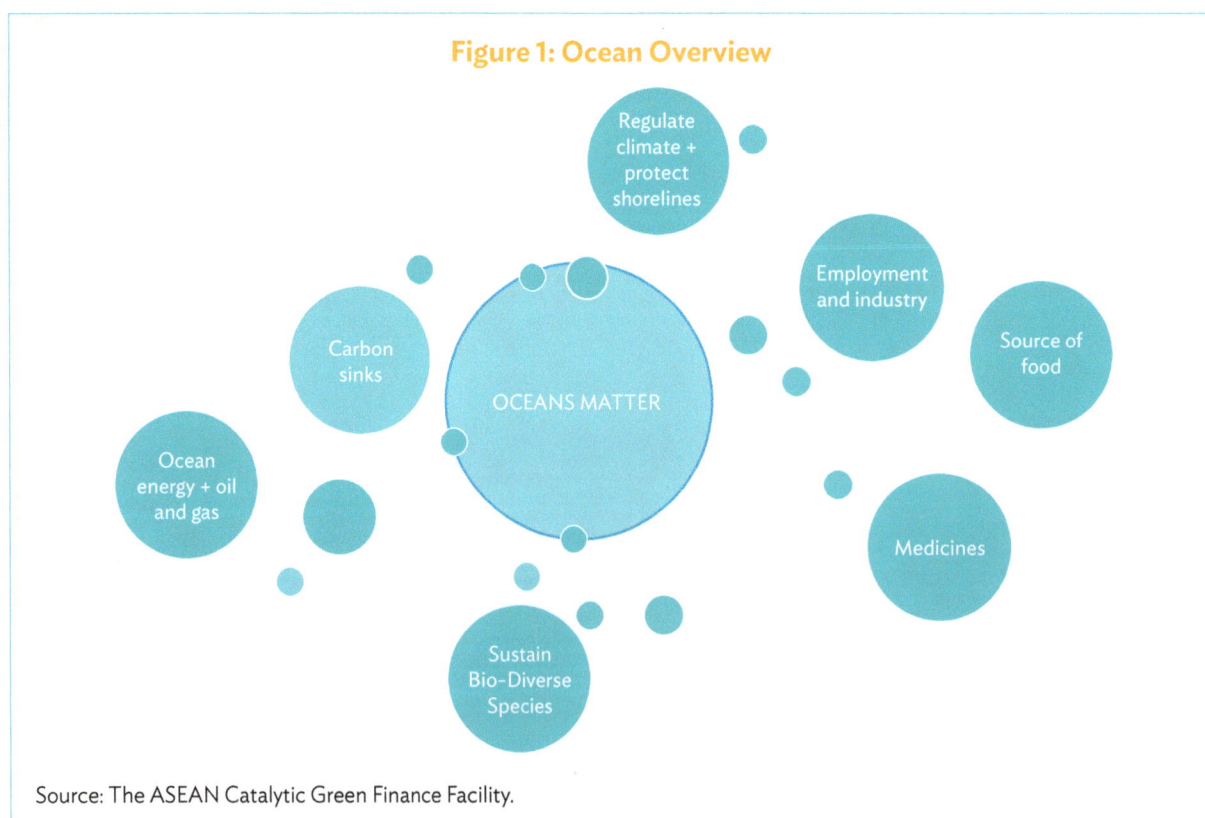

Figure 1: Ocean Overview

Source: The ASEAN Catalytic Green Finance Facility.

---

[1] United Nations Sustainable Development Goals. 2021. *Ocean Conference Daily Press Briefing by Damian Cardona Onses* (5 June 2017).
[2] Partnerships in Environmental Management for the Seas of East Asia (PEMSEA). Blue Economy.

The ocean's contribution to the world economy is often described as the "blue economy" and is defined by the World Bank as "the sustainable use of ocean and coastal resources to drive economic growth, improve livelihoods, while protecting and nurturing healthy marine ecosystems."[3] While there is no standardized definition of the blue economy, various institutions have given it distinct meanings. The Changwon Declaration in 2012, defined the blue economy as a "...practical ocean-based economic model using green infrastructure and technologies, innovative financing mechanisms, and proactive institutional arrangements for meeting the twin goals of protecting our ocean and coasts and enhancing their potential contribution to sustainable development, including improving human well-being, and reducing environmental risks and ecological scarcities."[4] The goal of the blue economy, as defined by the Asian Development Bank (ADB) is, "environmental, social, and economic sustainability of sectors that impact and/or derive economic activity from the ocean."[5] According to the Center for the Blue Economy, it "comprises the economic activities that create sustainable wealth from the world's oceans and coasts."[6]

However, in addition to the quantifiable aspects of the ocean's impact on our economies, perhaps of even larger impact is the unquantifiable impacts that the ocean has on biodiversity, climate, etc. One such key aspect is in its role as a carbon sink, which directly links ocean health with climate change, as shown in Figure 2.

The quantum of plastic waste entering the ocean every year is substantial and rapidly increasing from a previous estimate of 8 million tons in 2010 to about 19 million to 23 million metric tons in 2016, which constitutes about 11% of global plastic generation.[7] Undoubtedly, the issue of plastic pollution affects the health of our ocean but is also critical to the overall well-being of our planet.

Carbon dioxide (CO_2) uptake by the ocean happens through, first, dissolving of CO_2 in surface water and second, distribution through the circulating ocean currents that transport dissolved CO_2 from the surface deep into the depths of the ocean's interior, where it is stored over a long period. Scientists led by Nicolas Gruber, professor for Environmental Physics at ETH Zurich, estimate that this ocean sink has taken up from the atmosphere as much as 34 gigatonnes of human-made carbon between 1994 and 2007. This figure corresponds to 31% of all anthropogenic CO_2 emitted during that time.[8]

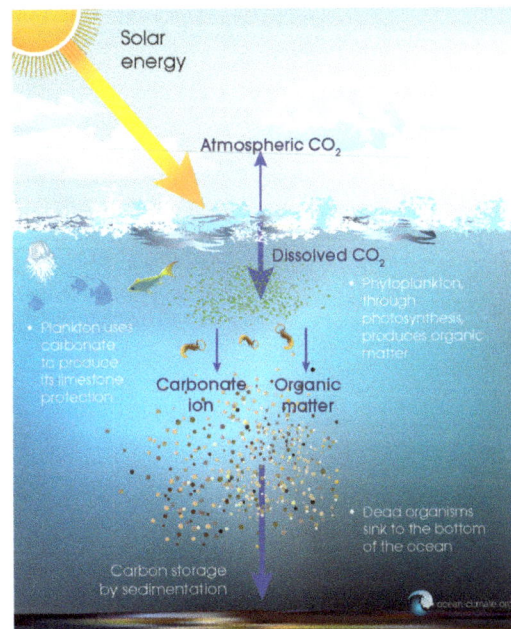

Figure 2: The Ocean, A Biological Carbon Pump

Source: Ocean & Climate Platform. The Ocean, A Carbon Sink.

---

3   World Bank. 2017. What is the Blue Economy? 6 June.
4   Fourth Ministerial Forum on the Sustainable Development Strategy for the Seas of East Asia. 2012. Changwon Declaration Toward an Ocean Based Blue Economy: Moving Ahead with the Sustainable Development Strategy. Changwon, Republic of Korea. 12 July.
5   *Development Asia*. 2020. The Role of Ocean Finance in Transitioning to a Blue Economy in Asia and the Pacific. 8 June.
6   Middlebury Institute of International Studies. Center for the Blue Economy.
7   Ocean Conservancy. The Problem with Plastics.; S. B. Borelle et al. 2020. Predicted Growth in Plastic Waste Exceeds Efforts to Mitigate Plastic Pollution. Science. 369 (6510). pp. 1515–1518. 18 September.
8   Science Daily. 2019. Ocean Sink for Human-Made Carbon Dioxide Measured. 14 March.

Furthermore, the importance of ocean health is recognized by the United Nations (UN) Sustainable Development Goals (SDG) through SDG 14: Life Below Water, which is focused on the inclusion of conservation and sustainable use of the ocean.

Southeast Asia. Looking into Asia and the Pacific, and in particular Southeast Asia, the health of the regional waters is of particular importance given the impact on lives, livelihoods, and climate-caused disasters. According to the Partnerships in Environmental Management for the Seas of East Asia (PEMSEA), the East Asian Seas (EAS) region is the center of marine biodiversity globally and is home to 31% of the world's mangroves, 33% of seagrass beds, and a third of the world's coral reefs. The EAS region countries and seas account for 80% of global aquaculture, 60% of the world's capture fisheries, is the conduit for 90% of world trade through shipping, and present a share of the ocean economy to gross domestic product of over 20% in some countries, as shown in Figure 3.[9]

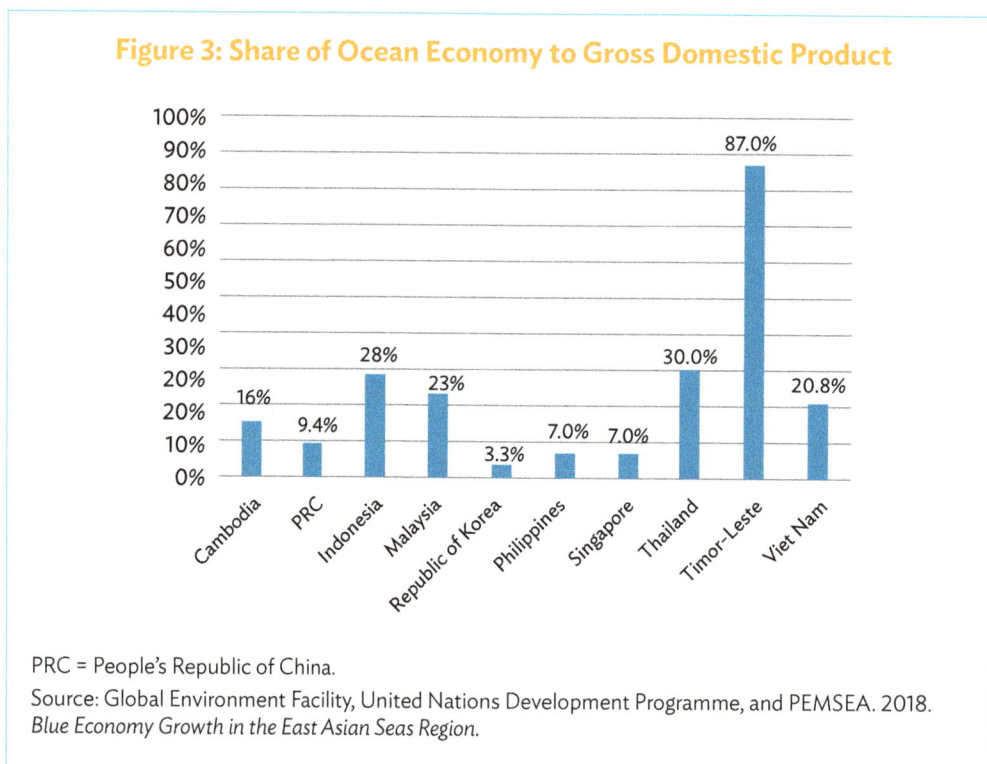

Figure 3: Share of Ocean Economy to Gross Domestic Product

PRC = People's Republic of China.
Source: Global Environment Facility, United Nations Development Programme, and PEMSEA. 2018. *Blue Economy Growth in the East Asian Seas Region.*

B. Ocean Ecocide: A Global Crisis

The ocean is falling sick from unabated human-induced pollution and climate-related factors. These factors pose a grave threat to marine life and humanity, undermining the productivity of our ocean, and include climate change, environmental pollution, unsustainable fishing practices, unregulated coastal development, and dumping of solid and liquid wastes.

---

[9] Global Environment Facility, United Nations Development Programme, and PEMSEA. 2018. *Blue Economy Growth in the East Asian Seas Region.*

A review of literature reveals the following predictions and likely impacts in the future:

(i) **Disappearance of seafood.** Seafood may disappear by 2048 due to overfishing and land- and sea-use change.[10] Overfishing has caused the largest negative impact on marine ecosystems in the last 50 years and could decrease the annual yield by more than 16% by 2050, if unchecked.[11] Illegal fishing costs the economy $36.4 billion annually and threatens the food supply and livelihoods of an estimated 2.6 billion people who are dependent on fish for an important part of their diet.[12] According to a World Bank Group report, adopting sustainable fishing practices could generate an additional $83 billion each year for the fisheries sector and improve global food security.[13] Further, $1 invested in sustainable aquaculture and wild-capture fisheries, is estimated to generate $10 in benefits.[14]

(ii) **Disappearing coastal habitats.** Coastal habitats are rapidly disappearing and nearly 50% of coral reefs have been lost in the last 3 decades. At the current pace, about 90% of this unique ecosystem will disappear by 2050.[15] The loss of natural coastal habitats is likely to increase the risk of floods and hurricanes affecting about 100 million to 300 million people living within coastal flood zones.[16] It is estimated that $1 invested in mangrove conservation and restoration is likely to generate $3 in benefits (footnote 15).

(iii) **Rapidly rising sea levels.** Sea level rise has more than doubled from 1.4 millimeters (mm) in the previous century to 3.6 mm in 2006–2015 and 6.1 mm in 2018–2019.[17] This acceleration in sea level rise results in more wetland flooding, destructive erosion, agricultural land contamination, and threats to marine habitats. Communities that live in low-lying coastal areas are and will be forced to migrate to higher ground.

(iv) **Increasing pollution.** Rising levels of pollution from the shipping industry is a major cause of disturbance in the marine ecosystem. Ships are responsible for roughly 3% of global CO_2 and greenhouse gas emissions every year.[18] If left unchecked, by 2050 the emissions are estimated to increase anywhere between 50% and 250%.[19] Shipping operations also produce waste in other forms, including ballast water, grey water, food waste, packing material, and cleaning material. Noise pollution generated by shipping operations, including vessel groundings, and cruise ship entertainment, can be detrimental to marine organisms and benthic habitat. Marine animals such as fish, dolphins, and whales are extremely sensitive to noise due to their heavy reliance on underwater sounds for basic life functions.

(v) **Oil spills.** Oil spills have caused significant marine pollution, harming and killing thousands of marine species, and damaging seafood and tourism industries.

[10] M. P. Rowland. 2017. Two-Thirds of the World's Seafood is Over-fished. Forbes. 24 July; S. Díaz et al., eds. 2019. *Summary for Policymakers of the IPBES Global Assessment Report on Biodiversity and Ecosystem Services.* Intergovernmental Science-Policy Platform on Biodiversity and Ecosystem Services (IPBES).
[11] C. Costello et al. 2020. The Future of Food from the Sea. Nature. 588. pp. 95–100. 19 August.
[12] WWF. *Illegal Fishing.*
[13] *World Bank.* 2017. Giving Oceans a Break Could Generate US$83 Billion in Additional Benefits for Fisheries. 14 February.
[14] M. Konar and H. Ding. 2020. A Sustainable Ocean Economy for 2050: Approximating its Benefits and Costs. High Level Panel for a Sustainable Ocean Economy.
[15] E. Becatoros. 2017. More Than 90 Percent of World's Coral Reefs Will Die by 2050. *The Independent.* 13 March.
[16] S. Díaz et al., eds. 2019. *Summary for Policymakers of the IPBES Global Assessment Report on Biodiversity and Ecosystem Services.* Intergovernmental Science-Policy Platform on Biodiversity and Ecosystem Services (IPBES).
[17] R. Lindsey. 2021. Climate Change: Global Sea Level. *Climate.Gov.* 25 January.
[18] Oceana. Shipping Pollution.
[19] European Commission. Reducing Emissions from the Shipping Sector.

(vi) **Pollution migration.** About 80% of marine pollution originates on land, mostly as a result of various human actions. Every year, 8 million tons of plastic mostly from Asia enter the ocean. In particular, Southeast Asia is a generator and victim of marine pollution from plastic. Four of the top five countries that are contributing to over 50% of the plastic pollution are in Southeast Asia.[20] As marine life eats these plastics, the pollutants work their way up the human food chain.[21] Moreover, discarded fishing nets and other debris harm thousands of seabirds, sea turtles, and marine mammals every year.

(vii) **Hazardous waste from mining activities.** About 220 million tonnes of hazardous waste is dumped into water bodies by mining companies every year. Bodies of water have become dumping grounds for solid wastes, untreated sewage, industrial waste, and construction debris.[22]

(viii) **Hazardous waste from agricultural activities.** About 40.25 million tonnes of nitrogen inputs from around 115 million tonnes of mineral nitrogen fertilizers used globally enter the ocean every year. Agricultural runoff and soil erosion from construction activities carry soil and particles that are mixed with carbon, phosphorus, nitrogen, and minerals into the sea, posing a serious threat to marine life and humans.[23]

C. Key Blue Economy Sectors

A healthy blue economy will benefit from the growth of numerous allied sectors. At the same time, it will take many other sectors to partner, develop, and launch investments to support sustainable coastal operations and marine activities. The cumulative investments needed for a healthy ocean is a sum of investments of respective blue economy sectors, and investments that need to be made across sectors. The financial strategies (including the choice of instruments), hence, need to be in accordance with the characteristics of the respective subsectors.

Investments in the blue economy have an opportunity to realize potentially attractive returns, while creating lasting social and environmental impacts. The investment blueprints from the report *Investing for Sustainable Global Fisheries* show that impact-oriented business models benefiting from fisheries sector stock restoration have the potential to generate equity returns between 5% and 35%, using conservative growth and exit assumptions.[24] These returns are driven primarily by increased volumes linked to fisheries stock recoveries, improvements in supply chain efficiency, access to higher-value markets, and reductions in supply volatility.

Most environmental sectors need public funding support for construction and operation and maintenance of infrastructure. The limited fiscal capacity of local authorities and the public sector proponents, particularly in developing Asia and the Pacific, have resulted in underinvestment in the blue economy sectors. There is a need to substantially increase the extent of investments to generate impact at scale required for meeting the ocean health-related commitments and also to develop sustainable, long-term concessional and innovative financing instruments.

---

[20] *United Nations Environment Programme* (UNEP). 2019. UNEP Report Warns Plastic Policies Lagging Behind in South-East Asia. 13 November.

[21] Plastic Soup Foundation. Plastic in Food Chain.

[22] Earthworks. 2019. Dumping by the Numbers.

[23] Food and Agriculture Organization of the United Nations (FAO). 2018. Pollutants From Agriculture a Serious Threat to World's Water. 20 June.

[24] Bloomberg Philanthropies Vibrant Ocean Initiative, Rockefeller Foundation, and Encourage Capital published a research report summarizing six investment blueprints, each intended to serve as a roadmap for investors seeking to deploy capital at scale and accelerate fisheries reform. A. Markham, T. O'Shea, and K. Wachowicz. 2016. Investing for Sustainable Global Fisheries. Encourage Capital, Bloomberg Philanthropies, and The Rockefeller Foundation. January.

1. Fisheries and Aquaculture

Of the top 15 fish-producing countries in the world, 8 are in East Asia, with exports valued at $136 billion. Asia accounts for 84% of all people employed in the fisheries and aquaculture sector worldwide and 68% of the global fishing fleet.[25] The proteins derived from fish and crustaceans account for between 13.8% and 16.5% of the animal protein intake of the human population.[26]

The fisheries and aquaculture sector comprise mainly private sector players of different sizes (small, medium, and large organizations), depending on the scale of their operations. This sector is perceived to have a direct effect on the marine economy, and the current blue initiatives are aimed toward more sustainable, traceable operations of these private sector entities. The smaller players are regional in nature, and operate in limited geographical areas, while the more organized bigger private sector entities have a presence across larger geographical regions. The investments in wild fisheries and aquaculture have very different risk-return profile, with the latter being one of the more popular blue economy investment opportunity.

The financing of these entities is largely commercial, and the revenue model is based on sale of processed or unprocessed produce. To promote sustainable fishing practices, governments are extending fiscal incentives, and the funding agencies and investors have been configuring newer financial instruments to encourage the same (such as blue bonds). The private investor community also influences investments through significant local community engagement, inculcation of better management practices in running the entities, and providing technological guidance. The public sector, in addition to policy, governance, and regulatory roles, undertakes capacity building activities for the small-scale fisheries and aquaculture entities.

2. Coastal and Marine Tourism

Travel and tourism generate $7.6 trillion annually—9.8% of total world GDP—and support 1 in every 11 jobs. As much as 80% of all tourism takes place in coastal areas, with beaches and coral reefs among the most popular destinations. International tourism in Asia and the Pacific has shown stronger growth than other parts of the world (footnote 25).

The sector includes hotels and resorts, cruises, houseboats, and water sport projects and related services. The characteristics of this sector are also similar to fisheries. It includes established revenue models (user fees or charges) and a large extent of commercial borrowings, with participation of the private sector. Public sector projects are usually selective and comprise beach management and heritage or cultural sites.

3. Waste Management

a. Liquid Waste (water, wastewater, storm water drainage, industrial effluents, agricultural runoffs)

The responsibility of providing water and wastewater sector services typically rest with the local government authority. In some instances, the authority may choose to provide them these services in partnership with the private sector (under public–private partnership [PPP] formats). The projects are typically financed with public sector funds and concessional loans from multilateral agencies. While the users are charged a fee, it is rare that the user fee is sufficient to recoup the capital and operations and maintenance expenditure. Usually,

---

[25]   Partnerships in Environmental Management for the Seas of East Asia (PEMSEA). Blue Economy.

[26]   Joint World Health Organization (WHO)/FAO Consultation on Diet, Nutrition and the Prevention of Chronic Diseases. 2002. Global and Regional Food Consumption Patterns and Trends. Availability and Consumption of Fish. In Diet, Nutrition and the Prevention of Chronic Diseases: Report of a Joint WHO/FAO Expert Consultation. WHO Technical Report Series 916. Geneva.

the public sector proponents offer a mechanism to increase the user charges or provide some form of viability gap support.

Industrial effluents and agricultural runoff management is the responsibility of individual enterprises and pollution prevention is monitored by the government. Various government agencies are attempting to configure innovative financial instruments that could aid in better wastewater management such as output-based aid, performance-related finance and microfinance.[27] However, there are no universally popular financial instruments. One of the reasons for the same include limitations in relating the receiving water body health to specific private actions on land or catchment area. The role of government continues to include policy formulation, governance, regulation (in some instances with an independent regulator), and capacity building. Fecal sludge and sewerage management are being undertaken with construction, operation, and maintenance of large sewer networks and sewage treatment plants.

b. Solid Waste (municipal, industrial)

In 2018, the United Nations Environment Programme (UNEP) estimated that plastic litter in Asia and the Pacific alone has a negative impact worth $1.3 billion annually on the tourism, fishing, and shipping industries. Cleaning up plastic wastes from coastal areas is also costly: the total economic damage to the world's marine ecosystem caused by plastic amounts to at least $13 billion every year.[28]

Municipal solid waste management (SWM) projects require substantial public funding support in many components of the waste management chain. The involvement of the private sector, either in management of the activity or through investment spans across the whole SWM chain: collection, transportation, recycling, treatment, and disposal, though the extent of participation varies substantially. These services are usually under contracts with local authorities. The investments made by the private sector are generally recouped through a combination of user charges and viability gap support in the form of tipping fees for treatment and disposal facilities, while there are instances of fully financed and managed private sector initiatives of recycling.

Waste–to–energy (WTE) projects, with different forms of waste streams being allowed, also require financial support that is extended either through higher electricity tariffs or a revenue support. Though multilateral development bank (MDB) climate finance has allowed for the adoption of WTE, the application remains contested for various reasons. The viability of WTE plants depend on a diverse range of factors including the waste characterization, the size, emissions controls that are mandated, and the revenue model including the power purchase commitments and any additional support required.

In Southeast Asia, the generation of municipal solid waste is substantially larger than that of industrial waste and e-waste (or emerging waste streams).[29] In some instances, it is mixed with other street sweeping and construction debris, leading to technical challenges of managing this mixed waste, and substantially affecting the project viabilities. Plastic waste management is a major concern due to the size and nature of the type of plastics (for instance, polymers like polyethylene terephthalate [PET] are substantially different than multilayered plastics or sachets). Though there are recycling and reprocessing options (packaging, carpeting, etc.), significant amounts of plastic waste still enter into water bodies.

---

[27] World Water Council and Organisation for Economic Co-operation and Development (OECD). 2015. Water: Fit to Finance? Catalyzing National Growth Through Investment in Water Security. April.

[28] UNEP. 2018. *Single-use Plastics: A Roadmap for Sustainability*.

[29] UNEP. 2017. *Waste Management in ASEAN Countries: Summary Report*. Bangkok.

4. Ecosystem Conservation

In general, the public sector is expected to take the lead in the preservation and management of biodiversity and natural resources (for example, mangroves and coral reef protection). It is also expected to undertake public outreach campaigns for adoption of best practices and compliance. The initiatives in this regard typically refer to policy measures, licensing provisions, setting standards, and monitoring compliance.

The benefits for project proponents are largely economic in nature, with limited financial returns in the short-term (i.e., generally less than 5 years). The financing method of ecosystem conservation includes public sector sources (with or without borrowings from multilateral or bilateral agencies), philanthropists and impact investors (for example, marine protected areas [MPAs]), and the blue carbon financing. The blue carbon financing and other credit systems, including biodiversity offsets, in lieu of free financing, and water credits are in the early stages of development. The business models and/or repayment capacities often do not meet the expectations by commercial private sector investors, even though some researchers have argued that the economic benefits (including avoided costs) far outweigh the financial gains.

Larger projects that are being configured by the public sector include area-based conservation, such as the establishment of sanctuaries and MPAs. These initiatives are expected to have significant economic benefits but are not expected to meet expenses through their own revenues. Nonetheless, some MPAs can become financially sustainable and provide return to investors, provided suitable revenue models and credit enhancement structures are made available. Investors usually provide up-front capital for the development of sustainable financial mechanisms and marine conservation needs. These types of projects are attractive to specific lenders such as impact investors as part of a blended finance setup. There is piecemeal, insufficient, and short-term funding for MPAs in the region; it is useful to explore innovative blended finance solutions for their development.

5. Other Blue Economy Sectors

The blue economy also comprises other sectors such as ports, shipping and shipbuilding, chemical and pharmaceutical industries located near water bodies, offshore oil and gas projects, marine-based renewable energy projects (coastal wind, floating solar, and tidal). The projects under these sectors have established revenue models, supported by commercial borrowing and market dynamics. Most of these sectors are dominated by the private sector, except ports, which have a significant public sector presence due to historical and/or strategic reasons.

The public sector intervention is largely in the realm of policymaking, governance, regulation, licensing, setting standards, and pollution monitoring and evaluation. Depending on the sector and the regional strategic importance, governments extend a slew of financial incentives and assist in or undertake research and development in specific instances (e.g., marine biotechnology in Australia, Brazil, and Europe). Public sector contributions are mainly provision of infrastructure (land, power, water, connectivity, etc.), the financing of which is through a combination of own resources, concessional funds, market borrowings, and in selective cases, PPP models.

PEMSEA's Blue Economy Report (footnote 9) highlights the industries listed here.

a. Ports, Shipping, and Marine Transport

Over 90% of world trade is carried across the world's ocean by some 90,000 marine vessels. Five of the top six shipping economies in the world are in East Asia, along with 9 of the top 10 busiest container ports (by volume).

b. Marine Biotechnology

The marine environment offers a new frontier of biological resources for developing a range of products from pharmaceuticals and chemicals to personal care products. Japan, Malaysia, the People's Republic of China (PRC), the Philippines, and the Republic of Korea all consider marine biotechnology in their public/governmental investment strategies and growth plans.

c. Oil and Gas

Asia and the Pacific's demand for energy is expected to increase 40% by 2022, and the PRC will become the world's top consumer of oil. Globally, offshore fields could account for 34% of worldwide crude oil production by 2025. The region will be the primary global buyer of liquefied natural gas (LNG) in the coming decade, requiring substantial coastal infrastructure.

d. Coastal Manufacturing

Asia and the Pacific accounts for nearly 50% of all global manufacturing output, half of which is from the PRC. The Southeast Asian region accounts for 7% of global exports, making it the fourth-largest exporting region in the world, from auto parts in Thailand to apparel and textiles in Viet Nam. The top three shipbuilding countries in the world are all in East Asia with the PRC leading the shipbuilding industry in 2020 based on gross tonnage, followed by the Republic of Korea and Japan.

e. Marine Technology and Environmental Services

A significant market need exists for companies providing marine technology and environmental services including oil spill response, environmental consulting, marine scientific services, and information technology (IT) and data solutions, among others. For instance, wastewater treatment technology and services are needed to address the 65% of all sewage in Asia that is dumped into the ocean without any treatment. IT-enabled solutions (such as remote marine surveillance and monitoring, drones, robotic fish, etc.) are needed for combating illegal, unreported, and unregulated (IUU) fishing, an issue costing an estimated $23.5 billion annually.

f. Renewable Energy

Technically exploitable marine-based renewable sources hold the potential to more than meet all current global energy needs. Governments in Asia and the Pacific are actively seeking ways to develop marine energy resources including wave, tidal, thermal gradient, and biomass.

D. Blue Economy Initiatives and International Perspectives

The recognition of the growing threats to the ocean have resulted in an increase in global "blue" initiatives. As a response to addressing the previously discussed threats, countries, organizations, financing institutions, and regions are preparing and pursuing strategies and action plans independently and jointly. A guiding framework for blue economy and the sustainable blue economy principles were developed in 2018 by a joint partnership of the European Commission, World Wide Fund for Nature (WWF), European Investment Bank, and HRH the Prince of Wales' International Sustainability Unit.[30] Efforts have accelerated in recent years to create sustainable fisheries, reduce litter and plastic from entering the ocean, and manage coastal development.

---

[30] European Commission, WWF, HRH the Prince of Wales' International Sustainability Unit, and European Investment Bank. 2017. *Introducing the Sustainable Blue Economy Finance Principles.*

Science, technology, policy, grassroots movements, and innovation will play a leading role in managing the development of the blue economy in a responsible and sustainable way.[31]

Selected key global finance initiatives in blue economy from MDBs, international organizations, and institutions are summarized in Table 1.[32] These international commitments indicate an agreed urgency for improving ocean health.

Table 1: Global Blue Economy Initiatives

Institution	Blue Economy Initiatives	Objectives or Focus Areas
Asian Development Bank (ADB)	ADB launched the *Action Plan for Healthy Ocean and Sustainable Blue Economies* for Asia and the Pacific in May 2019.[a] The action plan is supported by the *Oceans Financing Initiative* that will provide financing and technical assistance for ocean health and marine economy projects to $5 billion from 2019 to 2024.	• Protecting and restoring coastal and marine ecosystems, including rivers that drain to the ocean, through ecosystem-based management, nature-based solutions, and coastal resilience. • Reducing land-based sources of marine pollution, including wastewater and agricultural runoff, with a focus on marine plastics and circular economy solutions. • Building blue economies through innovative ocean finance, supportive enabling and fiscal environments, and the development of bankable ocean projects in fisheries, aquaculture, marine renewable energy, green ports, and shipping.
World Bank	The World Bank's Blue Economy Program PROBLUE was launched in September 2018 to support integrated and sustainable economic development in healthy ocean.[b]	• Providing financial assistance for the management of fisheries and aquaculture. • The threats posed to ocean health by marine pollution, including litter and plastics. • The sustainable development of key oceanic sectors such as tourism, maritime transport and offshore renewable energy. • Building the capacity of governments to manage their marine and coastal resources in an integrated fashion to deliver more and long-lasting benefits to countries and communities.

continued on next page

---

[31] OECD. 2019. Rethinking Innovation for a Sustainable Ocean Economy.
[32] UNEP Finance Initiative. 2021. Rising Tide: Mapping Ocean Finance for a New Decade. February.

Table 1 continued

Institution	Blue Economy Initiatives	Objectives or Focus Areas
United Nations Environment Programme (UNEP)	UNEP calls for the protection of the marine environment from land-based activities. UNEP has drafted a new Marine and Coastal Strategy of UN Environment Programme for 2020–2030 to set out the guiding principles for sustainable ocean actions.[c]	• Establish knowledge base on marine and coastal ecosystems to inform policy actions. • Build circularity in economies and promote sustainable approaches to address marine pollution. • Support policies and strategies enabling integrated management and sustainable use of marine and coastal ecosystem services. • Innovate financing instruments and initiatives facilitating sustainable blue economy transition.
United Nations Conference on Trade and Development (UNCTAD)	UNCTAD is supporting developing countries to identify opportunities and challenges in the ocean economy. It supports national trade and other competent authorities to design and create an enabling policy and regulatory environment that promotes the development and emergence of sustainable ocean economic sectors through the definition and implementation of national and regional ocean economy and trade strategies.[d]	
United Nations Framework Convention on Climate Change (UNFCCC)	The 21st Conference of the Parties to the UNFCCC, held in June 2017, resulted in including "ocean" in the Paris Agreement and paved the way for the subsequent Global Climate Action Agenda. The Ocean and Climate Initiatives Alliance brings together actors from all sectors and is founded on a strong science-based approach to adaptation and mitigation.[e]	• Blue carbon. • Marine ecosystem resilience. • Coasts and coastal populations. • Climate change and migrations. • Sustainable islands and small island developing states. • Science.
European Union's (EU) Blue Growth Strategy and Blue Innovation Plan	In 2012, the EU proposed the Blue Growth Strategy, specifying that blue growth will be the core of marine policies and stating key development areas and specific measures for the future. The Blue Growth Strategy has launched initiatives in many policy areas related to Europe's ocean, seas, and coasts, facilitating the cooperation between maritime businesses and public authorities across borders and sectors, and stakeholders to ensure the sustainability of the marine environment.[f] In 2017, the EU issued the Report on the Blue Growth Strategy Toward More Sustainable Growth and Jobs in the Blue Economy.[g]	• Pushing for growth in five focus areas: blue energy, aquaculture, coastal and maritime tourism, blue biotechnology, sea bed mineral resources. • The benefits of marine data, spatial planning and maritime surveillance to facilitate growth in the blue economy. • Promoting a partnership approach. • Boosting investment. • Making blue growth strategy fit future challenge.

continued on next page

Table 1 *continued*

Institution	Blue Economy Initiatives	Objectives or Focus Areas
G7 members, Fiji, India, Mexico, and Norway	The Ocean Risk and Resilience Action Alliance (ORRAA) was established in 2019 to build resilience in coastal communities and small island developing states (SIDS) that are vulnerable to risks from the ocean. ORRA also launched an Innovation Challenge to identify and nurture a pipeline of about 10 insurance projects that are viable, fundable and build coastal resilience.[h]	• Identify and develop strategies to manage ocean risk. • Drive investment of $500 billion into nature-based solutions by 2030, through innovative financial products (blended and private financing). • Develop a Coastal Risk Index with AXA XL, an insurance firm to calculate and measure physical and fiscal risks.
Civil society organizations, private and public sector financial institutions, and academia	The Coalition for Private Investment in Conservation (CPIC) was set up in 2017 to develop a framework and investment blueprints for conservation related investments.[i]	• The coalition established working groups to focus on the following areas: coastal resilience, forest landscape conservation and restoration, green infrastructure for watershed management, sustainable agriculture intensification, and sustainable coastal fisheries. • Serves as a hub for interested partners to connect and develop investable deals.
The International Union for the Conservation of Nature (IUCN)	The Blue Natural Capital Finance Facility (BNCFF) supports the development of bankable blue natural capital projects using blended financing models.[j]	• Drives investments in protecting restoring and enhancing natural ecosystems. • Facilitates access to debt, equity, and donor funding. • Offers grant funding or reimbursable grants for select projects. • Creates an investment pipeline and building investor confidence. • Monitors project impacts against social and environmental standards.
Willis Towers Watson (WTW)	WTW established the Global Ecosystem Resilience Facility (GERF) to develop resilience for vulnerable ocean ecosystems (such as coral reefs and mangroves) through innovative finance and risk management opportunities.[k]	• Develops and provides innovative risk finance (mostly insurance-linked). • Develops risk pools and expands potential for parametric insurance. • Provides alternative risk transfer solutions, such as catastrophe bonds. • Partners and participates in ORRAA.

[a] ADB. 2019. *Action Plan for Healthy Oceans and Sustainable Blue Economies*. Manila. May.; ADB. 2019. *ADB Oceans Financing Initiative: Accelerating Blue Investments in Asia and the Pacific*.
[b] World Bank. 2018. World Bank Announces New Global Fund for Healthy Oceans. 26 September.
[c] UNEP. 2019. Agenda Item 5: Consideration of Resolution of UNEP/EA.2/Res.10: Oceans and Seas—Proposal for a New Marine and Coastal Strategy of UN Environment Programme for 2020–2030. 145th Meeting of the Committee of Permanent Representatives to the UNEP. Nairobi. 19 February.
[d] UNCTAD. Oceans Economy and Fisheries.
[e] United Nations Educational, Scientific and Cultural Organization. 2017. Launch of the Ocean and Climate Initiatives Alliance. 24 February.
[f] European Commission. 2012. Blue Growth: Opportunities for Marine and Maritime Sustainable Growth. 13 September; and European Parliament, Library. 2013. Blue Growth: Sustainable Development of EU Marine and Coastal Sectors. Library Briefing. 6 May.
[g] European Commission. 2017. Report on the Blue Growth Strategy: Towards More Sustainable Growth and Jobs in the Blue Economy. 31 March.
[h] ORRAA.
[i] CPIC.
[j] BNCFF.
[k] WTW. GERF.

Source: The ASEAN Catalytic Green Finance Facility.

E. Southeast Asia: A Region of Crisis and Opportunity

Of all people around the world who work in fisheries, aquaculture, or seafood processing, 84% reside in Asia.[33] Given the wealth and biodiversity of its natural resources, the potential for a vibrant and sustainable blue economy is especially high in Southeast Asia. Within the 10 ASEAN member states, about 625 million people depend on the ocean for their livelihoods, significantly higher than most countries across the world.[34] The territorial waters of ASEAN cover three times the size of its constituent members' aggregate landmass, while the region plays host to 15% of the world's fish production, 33% of seagrass beds, 34% of coral reef cover, and 35% of mangrove acreage.[35]

The annual economic benefit per square kilometer of healthy coral reef in Southeast Asia (e.g., from tourism and coral reef fisheries) ranges from $23,100 to $270,000.[36] The ocean's economy as a percentage of national GDP in Southeast Asia is also substantially higher than that of developed countries.[37]

While there is widespread appreciation of the immense value of the region's marine ecosystems, more needs to be done in the region to protect this precious resource from further damage. Across Southeast Asia, intensive farming and aquaculture, rapid urbanization and industrialization, and the rising prevalence of plastic pollution are damaging the region's waters.

1. Intensive Farming and Aquaculture

As the global population increases, so does the demand for seafood and agricultural products. Intensive aquaculture practices and an increasing number of aquaculture farms have resulted in environmental issues: clearing of mangroves, species that escape from the enclosures that can or have become invasive, and pollutants in the form of dissolved nutrients, particulate nutrients, and chemicals (e.g., antifoulants, medication, and treatments).[38]

Agricultural waste has exacerbated the problem as farming in the region has increased in the past decade. Chemicals found in the water has led to an excess of nutrients, which in turn has contributed to rapid bacterial growth and significant damage to freshwater ecosystems.[39]

2. Rapid Urbanization and Industrialization

Many rivers in the region are highly polluted with household, industrial, and agricultural waste, lowering the Water Quality Index to unsafe levels.[40] Many of Southeast Asia's rivers contain up to three times the world average of human waste. This is primarily due to rapid economic development and urbanization. Areas within cities, which provide a range of benefits to urban dwellers, are increasingly becoming smaller and polluted. Problems such as flooding, and air and water pollution, are becoming worse in many places.[41]

---

[33] FAO. 2014. *The State of World Fisheries and Aquaculture: Opportunities and Challenges*. Rome.

[34] M. J. Spalding. 2017. The Association of Southeast Asian Nations' Role in Ocean Issues. The Ocean Foundation. 10 February.

[35] ASEAN Cooperation on Coastal and Marine Environment.

[36] ADB. 2014. *Regional State of the Coral Triangle—Coral Triangle Marine Resources: Their Status, Economies, and Management*. Manila. May.

[37] Ocean economy refers to economic activities that rely on the ocean directly or indirectly as an input to the production process or for producing a product or service. C.S. Colgan. 2003. Measurement of the Ocean and Coastal Economy: Theory and Methods. *Publications*. Paper 3. National Ocean Economics Program. 1 December.

[38] P. White. 2017. Aquaculture Pollution: An Overview of Issues with a Focus on China, Vietnam, and the Philippines. Washington, DC: World Bank.

[39] V. Tran. 2016. The Most Life-Threatening Issues Facing ASEAN's Ocean. *Cultural Vistas*. 24 February.

[40] *The ASEAN Post*. 2017. Southeast Asia's Stream of Polluted Rivers. November.

[41] J. K. Turpie et al. 2017. *Promoting Green Urban Development in Africa: Enhancing the Relationship Between Urbanization, Environmental Assets and Ecosystem Services – Msimbazi River Catchment, Dar Es Salaam*. Washington, DC: World Bank. 1 April.

3. Plastic Pollution

There are multiple paths by which plastic enters the ocean environment. One key route is river systems that transport plastic waste from inland to coastal areas and into the ocean. Nature Communications estimated that between 1.15 and 2.41 million tonnes of plastic flow every year from the global riverine system into the oceans, with 15 out of the 20 most polluting rivers globally in Asia, 7 of which in Southeast Asia.[42] As Table 2 illustrates, there is a high concentration of plastics in the region's river systems.[43]

Table 2: Most Polluted Rivers in Southeast Asia

Rank	River	Plastic Mass Input from Rivers in 2015 (tonne)	Cost of Clearing up Plastic Waste[a] ($)
1	Brantas (Indonesia)	38,900	58,350,000
2	Irrawaddy (Myanmar)	35,300	52,950,000
3	Mekong (Cambodia, Lao PDR, Myanmar, PRC, Thailand, Viet Nam)	22,800	34,200,000
4	Pasig (Philippines)	38,800	58,200,000
5	Progo (Indonesia)	12,800	19,200,000
6	Serayu (Indonesia)	17,100	25,650,000
7	Solo (Indonesia)	32,500	48,750,000
	Total Clean-up Cost		**297,300,000**

ASEAN = Association of Southeast Asian Nations, Lao PDR = Lao People's Democratic Republic, PRC = People's Republic of China.

[a] Based on estimate of $1,500/ton

Notes:
1. Data in yearly discharge predicted by the global river plastic inputs model.
2. Cost to industry is calculated based on the methodology used in A. McIlgorm, H. F. Campbell, and M. J. Rule. 2011. The Economic Cost and Control of Marine Debris Damage in the Asia-Pacific Region. Ocean & Coastal Management. 54 (9). September. pp. 643–651. The proxy of cost to the fishing and shipping industries were taken from S. Takehama. 1990. In R. S. Shomura and M. L. Godfrey, eds. Estimation of Damage to Fishing Vessels Caused by Marine Debris, Based on Insurance Statistics. Proceedings of the Second International Conference on Marine Debris. Honolulu, Hawaii. 2–7 April 1989. United States Department of Commerce. pp. 792–809.
3. Top seven polluting rivers in Southeast Asia, in yearly discharge predicted by the global river plastic inputs model

Source: The ASEAN Catalytic Green Finance Facility.

In this context, economies in the region have launched initiatives to stimulate a sustainable blue economy. The table below highlights a few programs in Southeast Asian countries in fisheries, ports and shipping, and tourism sectors, as well as actions to reduce pollution, restore habitats, conserve biodiversity and support climate resiliency.[44] A few regional projects such as the Greater Mekong Subregion Tourism Infrastructure project are also being configured. In almost all cases, these efforts have been financed by public sector spending, assisted in part by international organizations, as described in Table 3 and Box 1.

---

[42] L. C. M. Lebreton et al. 2017. River Plastic Emissions to the World's Oceans. Nature Communications. 8 (15611). 7 June.

[43] H. Ritchie and M. Roser. 2018. Plastic Pollution. *Our World in Data*.

[44] PEMSEA. 2017. *Blue Economy Forum 2017* Proceedings.

Table 3: Blue Economy Initiatives in Southeast Asia

Country	Blue Economy Initiatives	Financing Mechanisms
Cambodia	• **Sustainable tourism in Sihanoukville.** This includes zoning of beach for business area, green space, public access, and sanitation facilities as well as solid waste management. • **Sustainable port in Sihanoukville.** This involves implementation of the Port Safety, Health and Environmental Management System (PSHEMS) in the project site. • **Solid waste and wastewater management in Sihanoukville.** The project focuses on improving the garbage collection and landfill facilities, and the construction of a wastewater treatment plant in Sihanoukville. • **Sustainable Coastal and Marine Fisheries Project.** This project aims to enhance sustainable coastal and marine fisheries value chain and contribute to food security, and socioeconomic development of the Cambodian people.[a]	The Sihanoukville Project is part of the PRC's Belt and Road Initiative (BRI) Investment of $4.2 billion.
Indonesia	• Mangrove restoration and coral reef rehabilitation. • Ecotourism and marine protected areas. • PROPER program: This encourages compliance of industries to pollution regulations through an awarding or recognition system. • Green ports: PT Terminal in Lamong Bay has installed semiautomatic technology, which applies efficient sustainable practices for optimal performance and harmonious coexistence with the surroundings. • National Action Plan on Marine Plastic Debris, 2017–2025. • National Plastic Action Partnership.[b] • Sustainable and Equal Growth of Marine and Coastal Regions. • Establishment of blue economy demonstration zones in Lombok and Anamabs islands and Tomini bay for exploring the blue economy model featured with marine industry, fishery, breeding, seaside tourism industries, small island collective, regional, and bay development.	Mix of regional and national budgets, and supported by other programs such as "polluters pay principle" and strategic financing from international organizations and private investors.
Lao PDR	Wastewater management through the Fourth GMS Corridor Towns Development Project.	ADB grant of $48 million and sovereign fund of $6 million.
Malaysia	• Marine protected areas and ecotourism. • Green ports. • Sustainable marine aquaculture. • Sustainable fisheries: stock assessment; management strategies e.g., zonation, gear based, licensing, monitoring, and enforcement. • Alternative livelihood: seaweed cultivation; tourism. • Climate change response: National Coastal Vulnerability Index study. • Implementation of the Integrated Shoreline Management Plan; adaptation measures.	Mainly through regional and national budgets and tourism revenue.

continued on next page

Table 3 *continued*

Country	Blue Economy Initiatives	Financing Mechanisms
Philippines	• **Sustainable fisheries.** Work in this area includes amendment of the Fisheries Code; development of an ecosystem approach to fisheries management; establishing a 10-year plan of action to address illegal, unreported, and unregulated fishing; registration of fisherfolk, fishing vessels and gears; conservation of blue crabs and swordfish; implementation of closed season for sardines and small pelagic fishes; and banning the harvesting of sargassum and black corals. • **Sustainable tourism.** Initiatives in this area include preparation of the National Ecotourism Strategy and Action Plan (2013–2022); development of Zero Carbon Resorts and Green Fins program; MPA/tourism branding; promotion of marine and coastal heritage sites and parks such as theTubbataha Reefs Natural Park. • **Ecosystem conservation.** This includes initiatives such as the Mangrove and Beach Forest Development Project; the coral reef rehabilitation; the SmartSeas Program; and the MPA Network for sea turtles.	Public: national and international organizations and tourism fees revenue.
Thailand	• The Laem Phak Bia Project in Phetchaburi province aims to develop simple, natural, and low-cost wastewater and waste treatment models ideal for Thai communities. • The low carbon tourist destination project in Koh Mak, Trat Province uses alternative energy, waste management, and preserve traditional way of life. • The Bor Hin farmstay in Amphor Sikao, Trang province, combines ecotourism, mangrove reforestation, and the Seagrass Seeding Bank. • The Crab Bank Model in Chumporn and Surat Thani promotes education, stock assessment, and co-management with fisher communities.	Public: national and international organizations.
Viet Nam	• Mangrove restoration in Ca Mau and Tien Giang province (GCF). • Biodiversity conservation to respond to climate change (UNDP). • Green growth for 28 coastal provinces in Viet Nam (UNEP).	Public: national and international organizations.

ADB = Asian Development Bank, GCF = Green Climate Fund, GMS = Greater Mekong Subregion, Lao PDR = Lao People's Democratic Republic, MPA = marine protected area, PRC = People's Republic of China, PROPER = Program for Pollution Control, Evaluation, and Rating, UNDP = United Nations Development Programme, UNEP = United Nations Environment Programme.

[a] ADB. Cambodia: Sustainable Coastal and Marine Fisheries Project

[b] World Economic Forum. 2020. *Radically Reducing Plastic Pollution in Indonesia: A Multistakeholder Action Plan.* National Plastic Action Partnership. April.

Source: The ASEAN Catalytic Green Finance Facility.

Furthermore, the ASEAN has enabled regional policies and institutional arrangements to promote the conservation and sustainable use of biological diversity (including marine biodiversity) and fisheries. Through the ASEAN Centre for Biodiversity and the ASEAN Working Group on Coastal and Marine Environment, members coordinate actions within ASEAN and with other regions and international bodies.[45]

---

[45] ASEAN Centre for Biodiversity; ASEAN Working Group on Coastal and Marine Environment.

Box 1: Blue Economy Projects and Green Projects with Sustainability and Water Themes in Southeast Asia

The Green Container Terminal in Indonesia

The state-owned terminal operator in Indonesia launched its "green" Lamong Bay Terminal in 2015, a milestone in the country's sustainable transport strategy. The container terminal is part of the country's plan to improve the movement of goods through its waterways and result in better productivity. The terminal is designed to prioritize energy-efficient equipment, preserve the ecosystem, and promote environment-friendly business operations, through recycling, reforestation, and safe waste management practices.

The Lamong Bay Terminal is said to be the first green container terminal in the country and will increase the port's annual capacity from 1.5 million to 3.5 million twenty-foot equivalent units (teu). Once operational, the total capacity will be 5.5 million teu.[a]

Fourth Greater Mekong Subregion Corridor Towns Development Project

The Asian Development Bank (ADB), together with the Government of the Lao People's Democratic Republic (Lao PDR), provided funding of $54 million for the improvement of urban environmental services and the enhancement of economic connectivity along the Greater Mekong Subregion (GMS) in the Lao PDR. The project covers 1,600 kilometers of the GMS comprising 20 million residents and has the potential to generate more than $20 billion in regional output. The project will pilot the first decentralized wastewater system in the country.

Financing will cover sewage networks, wastewater treatment facilities, landfills, improved waste collection and management systems, improved drainage and riverbank protections and promote regional tourism and economic activity. The project is expected to be completed by the end of 2023 and the improvements aim to promote an environment capable of absorbing climate challenges.[b]

Tubbataha Reefs Natural Park

A study of investments into the protection of Tubbataha Reefs Natural Park in Palawan, Philippines, found a cost-benefit ratio of 1:8. By lowering costs to communities, management can be sustained, giving damaged and overfished marine ecosystems the chance to recover. The recovery of fish stocks within marine protected areas (MPAs) produces spill-over effects into the adjacent fishing areas, providing economic benefits to fishers, which can incentivize them to comply with the no-take zone rules of the MPA. Where reefs are allowed to recover, the improved health and biodiversity of these ecosystems encourage tourists to visit the area, providing potential income-earning opportunities for community members and local infrastructure development.[c]

[a] *Greenport*. 2015. Indonesia Launches Green Container Terminal. 26 May. https://www.greenport.com/news101/asia/indonesia-launches-green-container-terminal.

[b] ADB. Regional: Fourth Greater Mekong Subregion Corridor Towns Development Project.

[c] K. Hooper. 2017. Diving into Sustainable Marine Protected Area Management in the Philippines. *Solutions*. 1 March.

Source: The ASEAN Catalytic Green Finance Facility.

ASEAN member states have also economically liberalized their fisheries and fostered a single market by removing tariffs to enhance intra-ASEAN fisheries trade and investment.[46] Additionally, ASEAN has collaborated with the Southeast Asian Fisheries Development Center (SEAFDEC) to develop common policies. For example, ASEAN and SEAFDEC countries jointly agreed to a regional plan to promote responsible fishing practices in the surrounding seas, including the Sulu–Sulawesi Seas and the Arafura–Timor Seas.[47]

---

[46] ASEAN. 2012. ASEAN Sectoral Integration Protocol for Fisheries.

[47] Regional Plan of Action to Promote Responsible Fishing Practices including Combating IUU Fishing in the Southeast Asia Region

2 BLUE FINANCE: NEEDS AND CHALLENGES

Protecting corals. Divers remove crown of thorns around Datoy Island in Coron, Palawan, Philippines in an effort to conserve the coral reefs (photo by Brian Manuel/ADB).

"We consider the future of the new Ocean economy in the knowledge that the Ocean is already a significant generator of wealth."

A. Global Estimates

The ocean is valued at more than $24 trillion (Figure 4), and, if treated like a country, it is expected to be the seventh-largest economy in the world with an estimated annual value of $2.5 trillion in goods and services.[48] A major barrier to restoring and maintaining ocean health is increasing the access and volume of capital to fund and sustain projects, which most stakeholders agree is a fraction of the needs of the sector.[49] Public and philanthropic dollars alone are not enough to finance the sheer scale of required projects. According to McKinsey and Credit Suisse, much of the money coming into the conservation sector still comes from public sources, resulting in an annual shortfall of about 85% of the amount required.[50] Despite all the macro estimates, there is no current global or regional calculated finance gap that is universally acknowledged.

B. Southeast Asia Estimates

Studies by ADB indicate a total infrastructure (including land-based and ocean-based) investment opportunity of $3.1 trillion for Southeast Asia between 2016 and 2030.[51] Approximately, $1.8 trillion of the infrastructure identified in both studies can be assigned to green sectors, such as power, transport, and sanitation. This investment opportunity estimate is likely to be conservative given that critical green sectors such as waste management and smart city infrastructure are not included due to a lack of available data.

The study also projects that climate resilient infrastructure in the region alone would be $210 billion per year between 2016 and 2030. There is a financing gap of over 4.1% of GDP in 2016–2020 in selected ASEAN member states (footnote 51). The climate change adaptation and mitigation cost to make all these investments climate resilient over the period 2016–2030 is estimated to be $400 billion. Currently, the public sector funds about 90% of infrastructure development in Asia. It is clear, however, that neither governments nor MDBs can fund the investment gap identified without the provision of capital from the private sector.[52]

Looking into the blue economy, ADB estimated that the annual economic benefit per square kilometer of healthy coral reef in Southeast Asia (e.g., from tourism and coral reef fisheries) can range from $23,100 to $270,000.[53]

---

[48]   O. Hoegh-Guldberg et al. 2015. Reviving the Ocean Economy: The Case for Action 2015. Geneva: WWF International.

[49]   M. A. Vanderklift et al. 2019. Constraints and Opportunities for Market-Based Finance for the Restoration and Protection of Blue Carbon Ecosystems. *Marine Policy*. 107. September.

[50]   Credit Suisse and WWF. 2014. *Conservation Finance: Moving Beyond Donor Funding Toward an Investor-Driven Approach.*

[51]   ADB. 2017. *Meeting Asia's Infrastructure Needs.* Manila.

[52]   Marsh & McLennan Companies. 2017. *Closing the Financing Gap: Infrastructure Project Bankability in Asia.*

[53]   ADB, Coral Triangle Initiative, and GEF. 2014. Regional State of the Coral Triangle—Coral Triangle Marine Resources: Their Status, Economies, and Management.

Figure 4: Global Ocean Asset Value

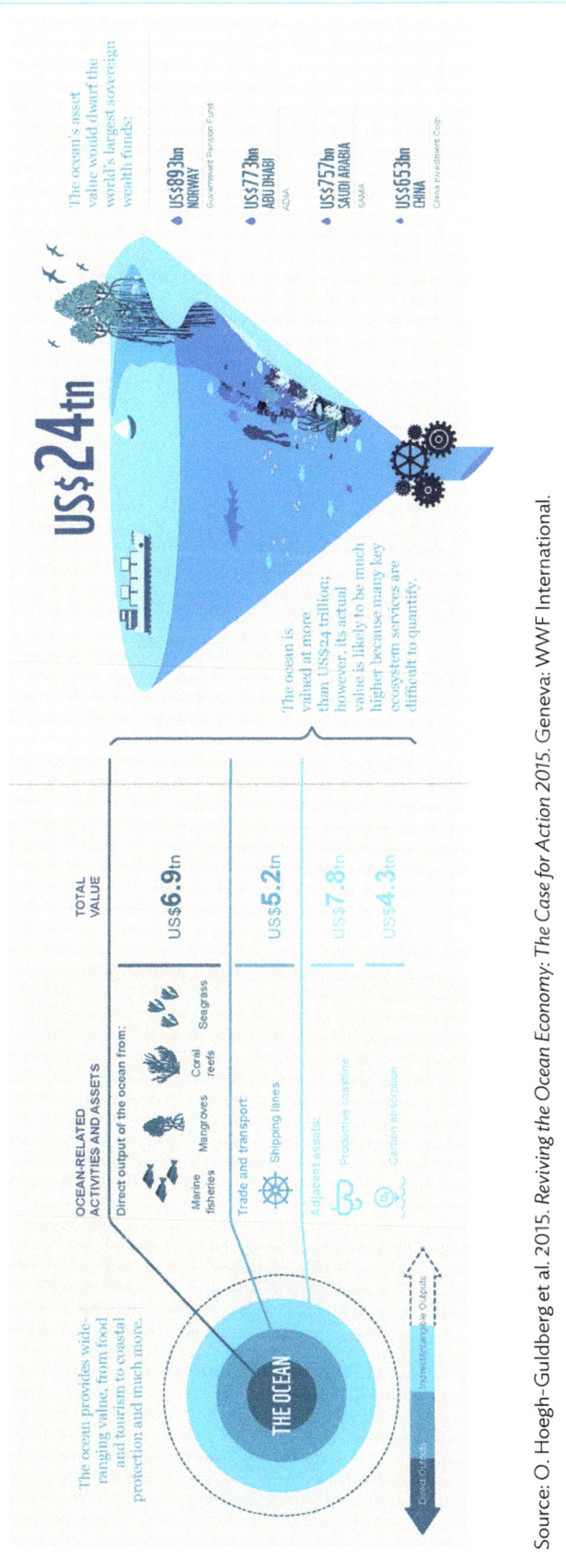

The ocean's asset value would dwarf the world's largest sovereign wealth funds:

- US$893bn **NORWAY**
  Government Pension Fund
- US$773bn **ABU DHABI**
  ADIA
- US$757bn **SAUDI ARABIA**
  SAMA
- US$653bn **CHINA**
  China Investment Corp

US$**24**tn

The ocean is valued at more than US$24 trillion; however, its actual value is likely to be much higher because many key ecosystem services are difficult to quantify.

The ocean provides wide-ranging value, from food and tourism to coastal protection and much more.

OCEAN-RELATED ACTIVITIES AND ASSETS

TOTAL VALUE

Direct output of the ocean from:

Marine fisheries · Mangroves · Coral reefs · Seagrass

US$**6.9**tn

Trade and transport

Shipping lanes

US$**5.2**tn

Adjacent assets:

Productive coastline

US$**7.8**tn

Carbon absorption

US$**4.3**tn

THE OCEAN

Indirect/intangible Outputs

Direct Outputs

Source: O. Hoegh-Guldberg et al. 2015. *Reviving the Ocean Economy: The Case for Action 2015.* Geneva: WWF International.

C. Green Lessons for a Blue Economy

Green finance is now widely acknowledged as a separate stream in financial markets and policy circles. The "green" label is a discovery mechanism that enables bond issuers, governments, investors, and financial markets to prioritize investments that address climate change and other environmental challenges that the planet faces today. Green finance denotes all financing instruments, investments, and mechanisms that contribute to a "climate plus" approach, impacting on both climate and environmental sustainability goals.[54] It promotes a reduction in greenhouse gases and improved climate resilience, air and water quality, ecosystems, biodiversity, and use of resources. These would actively promote environmental improvement, climate change mitigation and adaptation, and improve efficiencies in natural capital preservation and resource mobilization. A number of products would fit into this arena including green bonds, green banks, carbon finance, green insurance, green initial public offerings, green stock indices, green credit, and green asset securitization.

In the past few years, there has been an increasing demand from investors for investment opportunities that mitigate the risks arising from climate change, deliver social impact, and support sustainable development. The early learnings from green finance could guide development of the blue economy through the following:

(i) developing and growing the portfolio of innovative financial products on the lines of green finance instruments: green loans; green, social, and sustainable bonds (Box 2); green infrastructure investment trusts; and green index products;[55]

(ii) providing recognition from the investor base about the impact through more comprehensive disclosures;

(iii) increasing transparency and accountability in investments, primarily on the use and management of assets; and

(iv) enabling direct investments in the greening of traditional brown sectors, for example, through transition bonds.

Box 2: Lessons from the ASEAN Green Bond Standards

The following key elements of the Green Bond Standards could be applied to the blue economy financing initiatives:

- The issuer or issuance of the green bond must have a geographical or economic connection to the region.

- Information on the process for project selection and on the use of proceeds allocation, as well as the external review report, must be made publicly available on a designated website.

- Recommendation to obtain an external review for the green bond framework must be advised, particularly for the management of proceeds and annual reports.

- Recommendation for the external review providers must disclose their relevant credentials and expertise and scope of the review conducted.

ASEAN = Association of Southeast Asian Nations.
Source: The ASEAN Catalytic Green Finance Facility based on ASEAN Green Bond Standards.

---

54 ADB. ACGF Overview.
55 Climate Bonds Initiative. 2018. *Green Infrastructure Investment Opportunities Indonesia.*

D. Funding Constraints

Growing investor interest in environmental sectors is an encouraging sign. The green bonds market (comprising both the public sector and private sector issuers) had reached $290 billion in sales by the end of 2020, according to Climate Bonds Initiative, or an almost 10% increase from 2019.[56] Under the United Nations Framework Convention on Climate Change (UNFCCC), developed countries had committed to a public sector investment of $100 billion annually by 2020.[57]

However, financing generated from the capital markets or multilateral/bilateral agencies are not yet fully flowing toward ocean health and conservation efforts. Of the funds established by UNFCCC (Least Developed Countries Fund, the Special Climate Change Fund, the Adaptation Fund, and the Green Climate Fund) a study indicated that only 6% is in marine or coastal initiatives.[58] The financing options available for the blue economy are still in its early stages. The nature and characteristics of blue economy projects (with limited revenue streams, substantial investment requirements, and sustained development efforts spread across the project life cycle) imply that the financing options need to extend far beyond the conventional multilateral and bilateral aid to encapsulate multiple sources of finance including from private, institutional, commercial, and philanthropic investors.

The following are the key constraints for funding and recommendations to address them.

1. Measurement and Evaluation Considerations

The ocean has unique biological and physical features. Recovery of fish stocks, marine habitats, and ecosystems takes years, and returns may go to future generations. An interconnected ocean, which means environmental threats (e.g., pollution), migratory species, and challenges transcend Exclusive Economic Zones. The connectivity of the ocean raises issues and questions on responsibility and accountability, and consequently, on law compliance and enforcement. Much of the ocean still remains unexplored, making the benefits of blue finance even more uncertain. All of these uncertainties make it difficult for investors and sponsors to accurately estimate costs and revenues.

2. Bankability

A bankable project is generally defined as one that generates sufficient cash flows to meet obligations created during the outlay of capital. Investors and lenders are also looking for a project with a predictable revenue stream and they are often faced with projects that are not bankable or investment-ready. Banks do not make a project bankable (i.e., they have no influence on the ability of the project to repay the loan taken). Rather, their task is to assess the bankability of a project and, if found acceptable, provide the risk capital. The main concern for banks is the risk profiles of the project and, as such, the riskiness of their investment decisions. Unless a group of investors is satisfied with the risk profile of the project, they will not be willing to invest. Alternatively, they will seek various risk mitigations or credit enhancements that will only raise the total cost of the project.[59]

Analysis by Marsh & McLennan estimates that around 60% of all infrastructure projects in emerging markets in Asia are not bankable without noncommercial financing that often comes from public sources (footnote 52).

---

[56]   Climate Bonds Initiative. 2021. *Sustainable Debt: Global State of the Market 2020.* April

[57]   The Independent Expert Group on Climate Finance. 2020. *Delivering on the $100 Billion Climate Finance Commitment and Transforming Climate Finance.* December.

[58]   S. Guggisberg. 2019. Funding Coastal and Marine Fisheries Projects under the Climate Change Regime. Marine Policy. 107. September.

[59]   F. Rana. 2017. Preparing Bankable Infrastructure Projects. World Bank Blogs. 26 September.

The scarcity of blue investments can mean that it is challenging to accumulate a portfolio of commercially viable blue assets in projects belonging to blue economy sectors. Credit enhancement can help create an investment environment that mitigates bankability risk and encourages investment in ocean health projects. Credit enhancements aim to mitigate the specific risks of a project that either weigh on its overall credit profile or decrease its appeal to the private sector. Their effective use can lead to project debts receiving a higher rating compared to a scenario where enhancements are absent.[60]

3. Generating a Healthy Project Pipeline

Generating a healthy pipeline of blue economy projects is one of the most significant challenges that remain to be addressed. Progress has been slow on building a pipeline of projects that support a country's sustainable development goals while also being well-structured and bankable (or having the potential to be bankable). Scaling up conservation and development efforts will be challenging in the absence of addressing the pipeline challenge. Much of this work needs to happen at a national level and will be a critical part of creating the systematic transformation required to fully realize a sustainable blue economy.[61]

Establishing routine processes in project evaluation is a way to increase efficiency in the selection process. A due-diligence checklist for evaluating projects can help fund managers remove nonbankable ones from their pipelines early on to devote more time and money toward better ones. Project templates, such as Encourage Capital's blueprints for investing in sustainable fisheries or California's conservation-easement template, can accelerate the process of developing and structuring projects while helping investors avoid high-risk concepts (Box 3).[62]

The projects in the social and environment sectors have the conundrum—lenders and investors indicate there are not enough "bankable" projects, while the stakeholders on the ground and community feel that there is no money. Developing a pipeline of projects that meets the requirements of both the stakeholder

---

Box 3: Investments by Encourage Capital

Encourage Capital is an investment firm aiming for social impact as well as financial returns. In 2013, it began looking for opportunities to invest in fisheries governance reform. The firm began by building six investment strategies in Brazil, Chile, and the Philippines, in which private investments proposed small-scale seafood supply chain interventions. This, along with philanthropic investments in the local delivery of fisheries management services and the capitalization of community funds, formed the basis for wider reforms.

In the case of small-scale near-shore fisheries, the blueprints focused on philanthropic investments in community monitoring and the enactment of harvesting rules where legislation has defined the communities' right to manage access in certain areas. These sites would supply a hypothetical seafood processing company as the investable entity for the private capital, thus creating a sustainable sourcing network. The company would add value by investing downstream to reduce waste and targeting markets that would support premium seafood products that were harvested sustainably.

Encourage Capital has since made its first investment through Pescador Holdings, a holding company that has taken a stake in Geomar, a vertically integrated seafood company in Chile.

Source: Encourage Capital.

---

[60] M. Bariletti. 2019. Credit Enhancement: A Boost to Private Capital in Infrastructure? *World Bank Blogs*.17 January.

[61] World Economic Forum. 2019. *From Funding to Financing Transforming SDG Finance for Country Success*. 23 April.

[62] A. Markham, T. O'Shea, and K. Wachowicz. 2016. *Investing for Sustainable Global Fisheries*. Encourage Capital, Bloomberg Philanthropies, and The Rockefeller Foundation. January.

groups needs attention. The projects need to have desired environmental and social outcomes, as well as an acceptable revenue model with appropriate credit enhancements.

A closer, coordinated assistance to project proponents is required for developing a pipeline. The project proponents would immensely benefit if actionable sector and regional assessment is undertaken. These projects would need early structuring support to ensure that they adhere to the blue finance principles (discussed in the next section) and have broader access to investors providing funds to these projects. The projects need to be configured in a manner that can leverage blended finance sources and can access credit enhancement structures that are available in the market. Partially bankable projects can be accelerated to completion with such support. Specialist assistance for developing blue targets and frameworks can ensure that the blue principles are adhered to.

4. Inadequate Funding

Governments and philanthropic resources alone will not be sufficient to remedy the threats to ocean health on a global scale (Box 4). Revenue streams are not readily available or are currently limited for marine conservation, ocean pollution clean-up efforts, and sustainable blue economy activities. With concerns over mounting budget deficits and other domestic economic problems, governments are under increasing pressure to limit sustainable development aid.

Governments can impose taxes or charges for pollution as a source of revenue, but it is difficult for governments to know what the exact abatement cost is. Thus, pollution charges tend to be below this economic level, which is difficult to estimate. If pollution taxes are too high, polluters are being excessively penalized. The aim of zero pollution is likely to be unaffordable if the cost of pollution abatement exceeds the cost of the pollution itself. However, even sub-optimal charges are expected to have some positive impact on the behavior of polluters.[63]

Box 4: Blue Finance

Blue Finance is a social enterprise investing in the management of marine protected areas (MPAs). Through their investments, Blue Finance aims to create local economic development opportunities for vulnerable coastal communities while preserving pristine ocean ecosystems.

Good management of marine protected areas (e.g., biodiversity management, law enforcement) is critical to their effectiveness. However, over 60% of MPAs report inadequate funding to even provide basic services. Blue Finance tackles this funding gap by unlocking money from impact investors, development finance institutions, philanthropies, and de-risking partners to implement sustainable revenue mechanisms for the MPAs. Revenue streams are generated from innovative ecotourism solutions, nature fees, sustainable fishery, and blue carbon, which are pooled in a special purpose entity. This entity works with local governments and with local partners (nongovernment organizations [NGOs] and communities) managing the MPA under a long-term collaborative management agreement.

A portfolio example of Blue Finance is the MPA "Arrecifes del Sureste" in the Dominican Republic, covering 8,000 square kilometers and attracting over 4 million visitors annually. Blue Finance, partnering with local NGOs, signed a 10-year agreement with the government to co-manage the MPA. To finance the management, Blue Finance raised debt from impact investors blended with philanthropic grants. Through this investment, the MPA management is now able to create a marine spatial plan, improve and monitor the health of the MPA, ensure compliance and enforcement, engage local communities, support the MPAs tourism industry, and implement innovative revenue strategies to become financially self-sufficient.

Source: Blue Finance.

---

[63] Global Water Partnership. 2017. Pollution Charges.

BLUE FINANCE: PRINCIPLES AND MECHANISMS

A cargo ship docking at Danang Port. The Port is the third-largest port system in Viet Nam and lies at the eastern end of the GMS East–West Economic Corridor (EWEC), which connects Viet Nam with the Lao PDR, Thailand, and Myanmar (photo by Ariel Javellana/ADB).

Traditional ocean industries will need to mitigate the impact of their activities and adopt new technologies and sustainable operating practices. Industries need to align with climate-friendly, blue economy principles to maintain the long-term health, productivity, and resilience of ocean. Various investment approaches and opportunities that are available (i.e., multilateral and bilateral sources, market-based approach, incentives, regulations, etc.) need to be aligned for a cohesive development framework of the blue economy.

A. Existing and Proposed Principles

A key challenge encountered by blue finance is the lack of clear definitions and project selection criteria. Issuers and investors seek clear blue investment guidelines. In the absence of well-defined principles and a framework for "blue economy investing," investors will shy away from this sector. Standardization in terms of transparency, independent verification, and reporting is critical for building investors' confidence in environmental credentials and performance of the investments.[64] There is a need to develop generally accepted metrics that the investment community consider credible, evidence-based, and comparable across projects and investments.

1. Sustainable Blue Economy Finance Principles

Common standards coordinated and enforced by national and international bodies are critical to guiding investors in understanding blue economy investing. In 2018, the European Commission, European Investment Bank (EIB), HRH the Prince of Wales' International Sustainability Unit, and WWF launched the world's first global framework to finance a sustainable ocean economy.

The partnership found that for financiers investing in this complex and risky environment, there was little guidance available on how to act. The principles aim to promote implementation and achievement of SDG 14 and ensure that ocean-related investment delivers long-term value without negatively impacting marine ecosystems, carbon emission reductions, or the livelihoods of people who depend on the ocean and their resources.[65] The resulting 14 principles, which include 7 focused on sustainable investment and 7 principles specific to the blue economy, are designed to foster cooperation and communication on ocean health, scientific research, data collection, and technical innovation, according to the coalition (Figure 5).[66] UNEP FI now hosts the Sustainable Blue Economy Finance Principles and has launched a guidance document in March 2021 to assist financial institutions in screening blue economy projects, focused on five key ocean sectors connected to private finance: seafood, shipping, ports, coastal, and marine tourism and marine renewable energy, notably offshore wind.[67]

---

[64]   F. Rosembuj and S. Bottio. 2016. Mobilizing Private Climate Finance—Green Bonds and Beyond. *EMCompass No. 25.* Washington, DC: International Finance Corporation. December.

[65]   *WWF.* 2019. Pioneering Global Framework for Sustainable Ocean Finance Launched at Our Ocean Global Summit. 29 October.

[66]   European Commission, WWF, HRH the Prince of Wales' International Sustainability Unit, and European Investment Bank. 2018. Declaration of the Sustainable Blue Economy Finance Principles. May.

[67]   UNEP FI. 2021. *Turning the Tide: How to Finance a Sustainable Ocean Recovery: A Practical Guide for Financial Institutions.* March.

Figure 5: Sustainable Blue Economy Finance Principles

WE COMMIT TO APPLYING THE FOLLOWING PRINCIPLES ACROSS OUR PORTFOLIOS, REGARDLESS OF WHETHER WE ARE MAJORITY OR MINORITY INVESTORS.

1. **Protective:** We will support investments, activities and projects that take all possible measures to restore, protect or maintain the diversity, productivity, resilience, core functions, value and the overall health of marine ecosystems, as well as the livelihoods and communities dependent upon them.

2. **Compliant:** We will support investments, activities and projects that are compliant with international, regional, national legal and other relevant frameworks which underpin sustainable development and ocean health.

3. **Risk-aware:** We will endeavour to base our investment decisions on holistic and long-term assessments that account for economic, social and environment values, quantified risk and systematic impacts and will adapt our decision-making processes and activities to reflect new knowledge of the potential risks, cumulative impacts and opportunities associated with our business activities.

4. **Systemic:** We will endeavour to identify the systemic and cumulative impacts of our investments, activities and projects across value chains.

5. **Inclusive:** We will support investments, activities and projects that include, support and enhance local identifying, responding to, and mitigating any issues arising livelihoods, and engage effectively with relevant stakeholders, from affected parties.

6. **Cooperative:** We will cooperate with other financial institutions and relevant stakeholders to promote and implement these principles through sharing of knowledge about the ocean, best practices for a sustainable Blue Economy, lessons learned, perspectives and ideas.

7. **Transparent:** We will make information available on our investments and their social, environmental and economic impacts (positive and negative), with due respect to confidentiality. We will endeavour to report on progress in terms of implementation of these Principles.[5]

8. **Science-led:** We will actively seek to develop knowledge and data on the potential risks and impacts associated with our investments, as well as encouraging sustainable investment opportunities in the Blue Economy. More broadly, we will endeavour to share scientific information and data on the marine environment.

9. **Partnering:** We will partner with public, private and non-government sector entities to accelerate progress towards a sustainable Blue Economy, including in the establishment and implementation of coastal and maritime spatial planning approaches.

10. **Solution-driven:** We will endeavour to direct investments to innovative commercial solutions to maritime issues (both land- and ocean-based), that have a positive impact on marine ecosystems and ocean-dependent livelihoods. We will work to identify and to foster the business case for such projects, and to encourage the spread of best practice thus developed.

11. **Diversified:** Recognising the importance of small to medium enterprises in the Blue Economy, we will endeavour to diversify our investment instruments to reach a wider range of sustainable development projects, for example in traditional and non-traditional maritime sectors, and in small and large-scale projects.

12. **Precautionary:** We will support investments, activities and projects in our ocean that have assessed the environmental and social risks and impacts of their activities based on sound scientific evidence. The precautionary principle will prevail, especially when scientific data is not available.

13. **Impactful:** We will support investments, projects and activities that go beyond the avoidance of harm to provide social, environmental and economic benefits from our ocean for both current and future generations.

14. **Purposeful:** We will endeavour to direct investment to projects and activities that contribute directly to the achievement of Sustainable Development Goal 14 ("Conserve and sustainably use the oceans, seas and marine resources for sustainable development") and other Sustainable Development Goals especially those which contribute to good governance of the ocean.

Source: European Commission, WWF, HRH the Prince of Wales' International Sustainability Unit, and European Investment Bank. 2018. Declaration of the Sustainable Blue Economy Finance Principles. May.

2. Principles for Investment in Sustainable Wild-Caught Fisheries

Another set of principles that focus on sustainable fishing was launched at the World Ocean Summit 2018 from founding adopters: Althelia Ecosphere, The Meloy Fund, Encourage Capital, and others. The principles for investment in sustainable wild-caught fisheries are designed to provide investors with certainty about the specific challenges and enabling conditions in wild-caught fisheries, while also generating confidence that building environmental and social sustainability into fisheries will yield a strong return on their investment.[68]

3. ADB Ocean Finance Framework

ADB launched the *Action Plan for Healthy Oceans and Sustainable Blue Economies* (Healthy Oceans Action Plan) in 2019 to scale up investments and technical assistance to $5 billion between 2019 and 2024.[69] ADB created the *Ocean Finance Initiative* (OFI), which aims to: (i) define standards and metrics for ocean investments, (ii) develop a pipeline of bankable ocean projects, (iii) innovate financial instruments, (iv) mobilize public and private capital for ocean health and sustainable blue economies, (v) align taxes and subsidies with ocean health and sustainable blue economies, and (vi) enhance ocean finance capacity and build the enabling environment in Asia and the Pacific. The initiative is being piloted in Southeast Asia with support from the ASEAN Catalytic Green Finance Facility (under the ASEAN Infrastructure Fund), the Republic of Korea, and WWF. The OFI has developed an Ocean Finance Framework defining criteria for investments under the Healthy Oceans Action Plan, including disbursements from ADB funds, facilities, and innovative finance instruments. The framework is intended to provide transparency and accountability to ADB's external partners who collaborate and cofinance the implementation of the Healthy Oceans Action Plan.[70]

B. Blue Finance Mechanisms

With the billions of dollars required to support a sustainable healthy ocean economy, the current path of investment is not capable of addressing the magnitude of financing needs. In addition, the local authorities and governments would benefit from assistance in configuring large impact projects that can substantially achieve the blue targets (such as number and sizes of MPAs, amount of plastic waste removed, or river rehabilitation projects). These projects are likely to have limited revenues, but have significant social, environment, and economic benefits. The projects would require initial structuring support and a range of financing options at various stages—early stage, concessional and take out options (i.e., a costlier loan is replaced with a cheaper loan). Designing new financing instruments that provide finance based on the benefits accrued (or avoided costs), and that enable capitalization of such benefits might make the funding more sustainable.

There needs to be a holistic intervention with the participation of a diverse set of stakeholders for providing early stage financing, adoption of sustainable technologies and crowding in of private capital. Currently, there are initiatives by impact investment managers and innovative finance mechanisms that aim to provide proof of concepts. Opportunities in the blue economy are diverse, encompassing investments in green ports and shipping, offshore wind, water and wastewater management, conservation and ecotourism, and waste management and recycling.[71]

---

[68] Environmental Defense Fund, Rare/Meloy Fund, and Encourage Capital. 2018. Principles for Investment in Sustainable Wild-Caught Fisheries.

[69] The action plan was launched by the ADB President at the 52nd Annual Meeting of ADB's Board of Governors in Fiji. ADB. 2019. ADB Launches $5 Billion Healthy Oceans Action Plan. 2 May.

[70] ADB. 2021. Oceans Finance Framework. Upcoming.

[71] C. J. Clouse. 2019. 2019. Clouse. With Ocean in Peril, Investors Find New Ways to Invest in the "Blue Economy." *Impact Alpha*. 28 March.

1. Initiatives by Impact Investors

There are already ocean-themed impact funds targeting marine and coastal-based industries. Their objective is to finance coastal communities and marine environments conservation projects. Four of them are summarized in Table 4.

Table 4: Existing Ocean Financing Impact Funds

Fund	Objective	Size/Number of Projects/Duration	Investors and Partners	Key Terms
Rare's Meloy Fund (August 2017)	Incentivize the development and adoption of sustainable fisheries	$22 million; 10-12 projects in 10 years	GEF; Nederlandse Financierings-Maatschappij voor Ontwikkelingslanden N.V (FMO–Dutch Development Bank); Impact Investors; the Jeremy and Hannelore Grantham Environmental Trust; Bloomberg Philanthropies; JPMorgan Chase	Equity and Debt; Looking at Internal Rate of Return of near 6%; debt at 10%.
Encourage Capital	Investing for sustaining global fisheries	$100 million (hypothetical assumptions) across 6 blueprints	Private investors; grant foundations; multilaterals	5%–35% equity returns; around 10 years
Althelia's Sustainable Ocean Fund[a] (SOF) (October 2016)	Providing growth capital to companies that harness the ocean's natural capital[b]	$100 million across 10–15 investments	EIB, Axa, IADB, FMO, Conservation International; Environmental Defense Fund	Duration of 8–10 years with annual coupon
Circulate Capital Ocean Fund (June 2019)	Preventing the flow of plastic into the ocean in South and Southeast Asia	$100 million equity commitments from private corporations $35 million guarantee of loans secured from USAID	PepsiCo, Procter & Gamble; Dow; Danone; Unilever, Coca-Cola; Ocean Conservancy	Typical size of an investment is $2 million to $10 million Duration of 10 years + extensions;

ASEAN = Association of Southeast Asian Nations, EIB = European Investment Bank, FMO = Dutch: Nederlandse Financierings-Maatschappij voor Ontwikkelingslanden N.V. (Dutch Development Bank), IADB = Inter-American Development Bank, USAID = United States Agency for International Development.

[a] Althelia Funds.

[b] For example, Mirova (through the Althelia Sustainable Ocean Fund), IUCN, TASA, Blue Finance and ministry of Blue Economy of Belize announced their partnership in an innovative blended finance facility ($1.2 million) to improve the management of Belize's marine protected areas & contribute to its blue economy.

Source: The ASEAN Catalytic Green Finance Facility.

2. Innovative Financing Mechanisms and Instruments

Blended finance vehicles have a role to play, but more innovative financial instruments like debt-for-nature swaps, credit enhancements, social impact bonds, and blue bonds to tap regional capital markets could be explored to suit the needs of specific projects.[72]

a. Blended Finance

While there are many opportunities in the blue economy, few projects have an initial risk–return profile in line with those of institutional investors.[73] A blended finance approach is adopted to channel capital flows into the pipeline, implementing risk cover and credit enhancement to improve the bankability of projects when required. This approach can include investors from foundations, MDBs, impact investors, commercial investors, and governments (Box 5). Such types of arrangements can distribute risk between the public and private sectors and mobilize the needed private capital that would otherwise stay on the sidelines.[74] The various project phases will require different blending approaches. Blending solutions for the "construction" or riskier initial period will need to change for less risky financing required once the infrastructure project is completed. This would separate those forms of blended finance that would help with the riskiest phase (e.g., partial risk guarantees) from those that might help down the road (e.g., providing some first-loss protection on a pool of existing assets). As well as segmenting the blended finance, this fits with segmentation of the investors since some (e.g., many pension funds) would only consider operating assets anyway.[75]

Box 5: Blended Finance to Fight Plastic Pollution

The United States Agency for International Development (USAID) will guarantee up to $35 million of loans made by Circulate Capital to incentivize private capital investment and combat the problem of ocean plastic pollution in South and Southeast Asia.[a] The public sector support from the USAID partnership enhances the support from the private sector that Circulate Capital has received to combat ocean plastic, which is more than $100 million committed by corporations including PepsiCo, Procter & Gamble, Dow, Danone, Unilever, and Coca-Cola Company. At least 50% of the total investments covered by the USAID guarantee will be used for loans in Indonesia.

"By blending private and public sector capital, our partnership with USAID will accelerate and expand the magnitude of the impact we can achieve beyond anything we could do separately," said Rob Kaplan, founder and chief executive officer of Circulate Capital. "By financing companies, innovations, and projects that prevent ocean plastic in South and Southeast Asia, we will stop ocean plastic at its source and remove capital as a barrier to critical waste and recycling infrastructure development."[b]

[a] USAID. 2019. USAID Announces Private-Sector Partnership to Combat Plastic Pollution in the Ocean. 5 June.
[b] Ocean Conservancy. 2019. Circulate Capital, U.S. Agency for International Development (USAID), and Ocean Conservancy Announce Blended Finance Partnership to Combat Ocean Plastic Pollution. 5 June.

Source: The ASEAN Catalytic Green Finance Facility.

---

[72] Circulate Capital. 2019. Investing to Reduce Plastic Pollution in South and Southeast Asia: A Handbook for Action.
[73] OECD and World Economic Forum. 2015. Blended Finance Vol. 1: A Primer for Development Finance and Philanthropic Funders. September.
[74] R. MacFarlane. 2019. Marine Litter Problem is Solvable With a Little Help. Bloomberg Law. 10 June.
[75] Brookings Institute, Global Economy, and Development at Brookings. 2017. G20 Brainstorming Workshop: Mobilizing Private Finance for Sustainable Infrastructure. Buenos Aires, Argentina. 7–8 September.

b. Credit Enhancements

Credit-enhancement arrangements answer to the demand to mitigate the risks of the project and attract further financing and investment to the project. It is a de-risking mechanism that seeks to reduce the credit risk of the financeable aspects of a project.

MDBs offer a portion of the loan while attracting other lenders to join in other tranches (Figure 6). The MDB will be the lender-of-record, lead lender, and administrative agent in the transaction. The benefit to the additional lenders is that it reduces part of the risks of the operations by also being covered by the "umbrella" of the MDBs that include a preferred creditor status. Often, these mechanisms are used in combination (with each other or other financing schemes) to achieve a more effective project.[76] This was exemplified in the Seychelles Blue Bond, which was supported by the World Bank and the Global Environment Facility (GEF). The World Bank provided a $5 million grant to guarantee the bond, and GEF a $5 million loan to subsidize payment of the bond coupons.

The Office of the Pacific Ocean Commissioner has published the contours of the three Pacific bonds in 2020: the Pacific Ocean Impact Bond, the Pacific Ocean Resilience Bond, and the Pacific Ocean Climate Mitigation Bond, which vary in their application, designs, and provide flexibility to cater to the needs of the participating nations.[77]

Figure 6: Pacific Ocean Bond Concept from the Pacific Ocean Finance Program

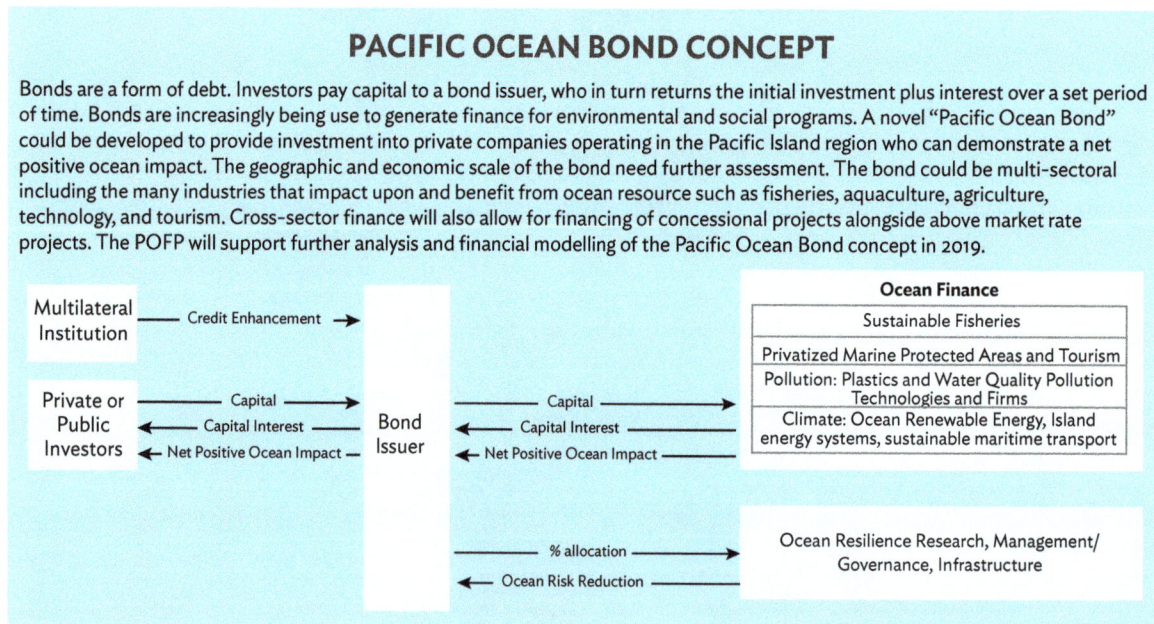

PACIFIC OCEAN BOND CONCEPT

Bonds are a form of debt. Investors pay capital to a bond issuer, who in turn returns the initial investment plus interest over a set period of time. Bonds are increasingly being use to generate finance for environmental and social programs. A novel "Pacific Ocean Bond" could be developed to provide investment into private companies operating in the Pacific Island region who can demonstrate a net positive ocean impact. The geographic and economic scale of the bond need further assessment. The bond could be multi-sectoral including the many industries that impact upon and benefit from ocean resource such as fisheries, aquaculture, agriculture, technology, and tourism. Cross-sector finance will also allow for financing of concessional projects alongside above market rate projects. The POFP will support further analysis and financial modelling of the Pacific Ocean Bond concept in 2019.

POFP = Pacific Ocean Finance Program.

Source: M. Walsh. 2018. Finance for Pacific Ocean Governance Part 1: Background. Pacific Ocean Finance Program, Office of the Pacific Ocean Commissioner, and Pacific Island Forum Fisheries Agency.

[76] M. Ruete, M. Aravamuthan, and C. Dominguez. 2015. *Credit Enhancement for Green Projects: Promoting Credit-Enhanced Financing from Multilateral Development Banks for Green Infrastructure Financing.* International Institute for Sustainable Development.

[77] Office of the Pacific Ocean Commissioner. 2020. *Analysis & Development of a Pacific Ocean Bond.* Pacific Ocean Finance Reports.

c. Debt Restructuring and Debt-for-Nature Swaps

Banks, governments, and lending institutions held more than $184 trillion in loans to developing countries in 2017.[78] There is little prospect of ever collecting much of this debt, and banks are often willing to sell bonds at a steep discount—as little as $0.10 on the dollar. Conservation organizations can buy these debt obligations on the secondary market at a discount and then offer to cancel the debt if the debtor country agrees to protect or restore an area of ocean health importance.[79]

Debt-for-nature swaps present a potential avenue through which debt can be reduced and complementary funds raised for important conservation activities. Some of the drawbacks have been identified, such as the relatively small amounts of actual debt relief and potential high transaction costs, particularly financial and legal fees, where there may be a need to issue new instruments to refinance the loan (buyback). Typically, this instrument has been used following a debt-restructuring process. The combination of public and private funds also creates a new model for co-investment debt swaps in small island developing states (SIDS). The Nature Conservancy initiative is aimed at debt restructuring of many island nations through the blue bonds initiative.[80]

The World Bank has proposed a debt-for-nature and resilience financing facility for small states.[81] The facility proposes to retire high-cost commercial or bilateral debt, such that the savings from the debt reduction creates additional fiscal space, which can be used to finance current or capital expenditure. The qualifying criteria include:

(i)   willingness to implement policy and institutional reforms for environmental management and climate resilience;
(ii) identification of debt that could be bought back, preferably at a discount and/or replaced by cheaper and longer-maturity debt; and
(iii) identification of a donor/or donors who can provide additional funds for the debt buyback operation (in exchange for policy reforms).

Similarly, the Commonwealth Secretariat developed a proposal for a debt-for-climate swap facility for small vulnerable economies, many of which are SIDS.[82] This facility could potentially mobilize up to $4.5 billion in additional financing for climate change adaptation across all SIDS. In addition, the United Nations Development Programme (UNDP) proposed "multi-creditor" debt swaps as a tool to reduce heavy transaction costs and maximize development impact. Additionally, the United Nations Economic Commission for Latin America and the Caribbean (ECLAC) is exploring the potential for climate finance pledges to be used to write down the high debt of Caribbean countries in exchange for investments in climate adaptation and mitigation by those countries.[83]

d. Environmental Impact Bonds and Development Impact Bonds

Environmental impact bonds (Figure 7) and development impact bonds are forms of payment-for-results schemes based on a PPP arrangement between governments (or donors in the case of the development impact bonds), and the private and nonprofit sectors to deliver projects with a particular social or environmental objective. They are not bonds in the traditional sense (i.e., offer a fixed rate of return and

---

[78] S. Mbaye and M. M. Badia. 2019. New Data on Global Debt. *International Monetary Fund* (IMF) Blog. 2 January.

[79] W. Cunningham and M. Cunningham. 2016. *Principle of Environmental Science: Inquiry and Applications.* The McGraw Hill Companies.

[80] The Nature Conservancy. 2016. *Rising Tides: Debt-for-Nature Swaps Let Impact Investors Finance Climate Resilience.* 17 June.

[81] OECD and The World Bank. 2016. *Climate and Disaster Resilience Financing in Small Island Developing States.* 10 November.

[82] The Commonwealth. 2016. *Discussion Note Commonwealth. Unlocking Climate Finance for Commonwealth Countries.* October.

[83] Caribbean Development Bank. 2018. *Financing the Blue Economy: A Caribbean Development Opportunity.* 31 May.

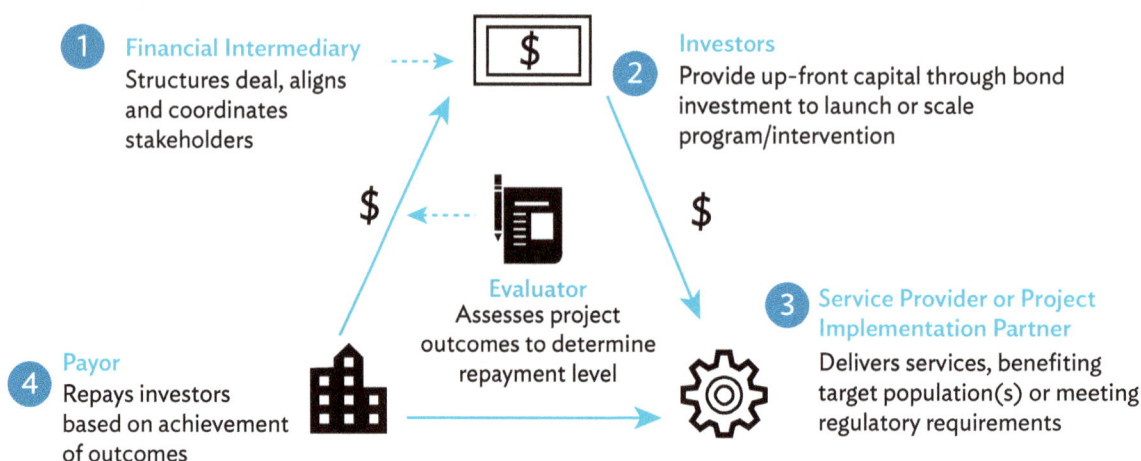

Figure 7: What Is an Environmental Impact Bond?

1. **Financial Intermediary** Structures deal, aligns and coordinates stakeholders

2. **Investors** Provide up-front capital through bond investment to launch or scale program/intervention

Evaluator Assesses project outcomes to determine repayment level

3. **Service Provider or Project Implementation Partner** Delivers services, benefiting target population(s) or meeting regulatory requirements

4. **Payor** Repays investors based on achievement of outcomes

Source: *Environmental Defense Fund*. 2018. Environmental Impact Bonds: Financing for Wetlands Restoration.

repayment of principal on maturity). The features of such bonds are varied. Some Development Impact Bonds (e.g., DC Water) have been issued in tax exempt municipal bond form, whereas other impact bonds are redeemed by the investor only if specified social or environmental outcomes are achieved.[84]

Impact bonds typically involve three key actors:

(i) investors who provide up-front capital for the project;
(ii) service providers who implement the project; and
(iii) outcome funders (also known as payors) who return the capital to the original investor(s), plus a small return in the event of success (outcome funders can be donors, philanthropists, or national authorities).

Environmental impact bonds and development impact bonds have been used to fund interventions such as tackling youth unemployment; tackling recidivism; and increasing biodiversity (Box 6). These instruments are typically better suited to smaller, well-targeted and bespoke interventions, and can have high transaction costs relative to their small size. This financing tool is still relatively new to most developing economies. With respect to the blue economy, this financing model may have several applications, which warrant further exploration. Among the potential applications includes assistance to waste management stakeholders in increased fee collection; promotion of waste reduction; strengthening waste collection and transportation; improvement in infrastructure design efficiency; defrayed risk for investors and resulting increase in investments.[85]

Significant lead time is required to prepare clearly defined and quantifiable performance metrics that are used to trigger payments to the initial funder. Lead time is also required to put in place the mix of partners needed (i.e., private sector provider of the up-front capital; project implementation partner(s); independent

[84] United States Environmental Protection Agency, Water Infrastructure and Resiliency Finance Center. 2017. *DC Water's Environmental Impact Bond: A First of its Kind*. April.

[85] S. Kaza et al. 2018. *What a Waste 2.0: A Global Snapshot of Solid Waste Management to 2050*. Washington, DC: World Bank.

Box 6: First Environmental Impact Bond in the United States

The Forest Resilience Bond aims to measure and monetize the benefits of forest restoration in the western United States to provide a return to investors.

Why forest restoration? Much of the western United States has been exposed to serious wildfires over the past several decades. These fires have been exacerbated by above-average drought in many areas of the nation.

Spending by the United States Forest Service (USFS) to combat these fires has increased from 17% to 51% in just 20 years. Usually, these methods entail fire suppression, which leads to a lot of build-up and growth in forests that would normally burn up. USFS spending on fire suppression leads to less money for wildfire prevention, creating a vicious cycle that Blue Forest Conservation is aiming to disrupt.

This bond helps align the incentives of USFS and other beneficiaries, such as water and electric utilities, to share in forest restoration costs just as they share in benefits. These benefits include reduced fire severity and augmented water flow. Investor capital is raised to fund treatments that are in line with USFS policy up front to restore forests to a natural state so that they are less susceptible to these fires. It's a preventative approach. The bond then uses pay-for-success contracts that enable the multiple beneficiaries to repay investors with a portion of the independently measured and verified results.

In California alone, the project is aiming to take a watershed-by-watershed approach in an effort to deploy over $1.5 billion for forest restoration. Investor return comes from a combination of increasing and monetizing greater water yield, increasing the provision of hydroelectricity due to greater water flow, and reducing the costs of fire suppression. There are also tangible social benefits, including job creation and reduced risk of property and crop damage in wildfire-prone areas.

Source: L. Yonavjak. 2016. Environmental Impact Bonds Pay for Performance. Conservation Finance Network. 12 January.

performance evaluator; outcome funder(s)—which could be an official donor or the national government, or both). Given the complexity of these bonds, many investors use intermediaries to structure and oversee the contracts on their behalf. Nevertheless, this financing model may offer opportunities to fund smaller niche interventions which could otherwise be left unfunded.

e. Blue Bonds

A blue bond is an innovative ocean financing instrument whereby proceeds of bonds raised are earmarked exclusively for projects deemed ocean-friendly (Boxes 7, 8, 9).[86] The Seychelles Blue Bond was the first sovereign issued bond that attracted the attention of the stakeholders.[87] Other blue bonds followed in 2019 with the blue bonds issuance of $10 million from Morgan Stanley and the World Bank aiming to solve the challenge of plastic waste pollutions.[88] ADB issued its first ever dual-tranche blue bonds in September 2021 to finance ocean-related projects in Asia in the Pacific (see Box 10). Innovative blue financing tools, such as blue bonds in partnership with blended financing mechanism, can provide the much-needed financing to support ocean economy. The combined tools resulted in a reduction in borrowing rate as can be seen in the Seychelles Blue Bond model (from 6% to 2.5%).

[86] M. Ahmed. 2019. Blue Bonds: What They Are, and How They Can Help the Oceans. World Economic Forum. 6 June.
[87] World Bank. 2018. Seychelles Launches World's First Sovereign Blue Bond. 29 October.
[88] World Bank. 2019. World Bank Launched Bonds to Highlight the Challenge of Plastic Waste in Oceans. 3 April.

Box 7: Seychelles Blue Bond

Seychelles issued the world's first sovereign blue bond as a means to attract private capital firms to invest in sustainable fisheries management. The bond emanates from a debt buyback and refinancing of an existing debt of $22 million with Paris Club creditors in February 2016.

The bond was issued at a nominal amount of $15 million with a 10-year maturity period, partially guaranteed by a $5 million guarantee from the World Bank (International Bank for Reconstruction and Development) and further supported by a $5 million concessional loan from the Global Environment Facility, which will partially cover interest payments for the bond. This will help reduce risk to investors and subsequently lower the interest rate to around 2.5%.

Proceeds of the blue bond will be used as grants for fisheries management planning activities and as loans to encourage local public and private investment in activities consistent with sustainable fishing, such as post-harvest value-adding opportunities, jobs and the protection of ocean resources. The blue bond proceeds will be disbursed on a competitive basis through the Seychelles Conservation and Climate Adaptation Trust and the Development Bank of Seychelles.

Source: *World Bank*. 2018. Seychelles Launches World's First Sovereign Blue Bond. 29 October.

Box 8: Nordic–Baltic Blue Bond

In 2019, the Nordic Investment Bank (NIB) issued its first Nordic–Baltic Blue Bond with Skandinaviska Enskilda Banken AB (SEB) as the lead manager. The 5-year, $213 million bond is targeted to finance wastewater treatment, prevention of water pollution and water-related climate change adaptation. The bond offering 3.75% coupon was oversubscribed more than two times demonstrates the interest by impact investors when presented with a well-structured financial investment vehicle.

Source: *NIB*. 2019. NIB Issues first Nordic–Baltic Blue Bond. 24 January.

Box 9: Bonds for Species Conservation: Rhino Impact Bond

The $50 million Rhino Impact Bonds (RIB) will be the world's first financial instrument working toward the conservation of a species at the risk of extinction, which could be replicated for marine species. The bond, which was expected to launch in the first quarter of 2020, aims to boost the black rhino population by 10% globally.

The bond (a fixed-income investment instrument) has a 5-year term and is targeting growing the numbers of African black rhinos across five sites in Kenya and South Africa. It covers a total of 700 black rhinos that form about 12% of the world's entire black rhino population.

Transferring the risk of funding conservation from donors to impact investors by linking conservation performance to financial performance "outcome payments" model—a concept where investors receive financial returns only on the successful and measurable completion of the objective.

Investors will pay an upfront cost for buying the bond and they will be paid back their capital and a coupon if the population of African black rhinos increases in 5 years. The yield on the bond will be subject to the growth of the rhino population.

Source: A. Sguazzin. 2021. World's First Wildlife Bond to Track Rhino Numbers in Africa. *Bloomberg Quint*. 24 March.

Box 10: ADB Issues First Blue Bond for Ocean Investments

In September 2021, ADB issued its first ever dual-tranche blue bonds denominated in Australian and New Zealand dollars that will finance ocean-related projects in Asia and the Pacific. The bonds are part of ADB's Action Plan for Healthy Oceans and Sustainable Blue Economies launched in 2019, which aims to catalyze sustainable investments in Asia and the Pacific by committing to invest and provide technical assistance of at least $5 billion by 2024.

The A$208 million (around $151 million) 15-year issue was purchased by The Dai-chi Life Insurance Company and arranged by Citigroup Global Markets Limited. The NZ$217 million (around $151 million) 10-year issue was purchased by Meiji Yasuda Life Insurance Company and arranged by Credit Agricole CIB. The bonds were issued under ADB's expanded Green and Blue Bond Framework which received a Second Party Opinion from the leading evaluator of green bond investment frameworks CICERO Shades of Green. This provides investors with confidence that ADB bonds are mitigating climate change and protecting ocean health.

An example of an eligible project that may be financed by the bond is the Greater Malé Waste-to-Energy Project in Maldives, which will stem the flow of plastics and other wastes to the ocean and reduce greenhouse gas emissions. Another is the Anhui Huangshan Xin'an River Ecological Protection and Green Development Project in the People's Republic of China which will reduce non-point source pollution to the marine environment from "source to sea" by supporting green farming and controlling pesticide and fertilizer use.

Source: Asian Development Bank.

Nonetheless, the support of the public sector players such as MDBs is essential in this structure. To catalyze private capital market investors to invest, a de-risking mechanism needs to be in place to provide investors' confidence. Table 5 presents launched blue bonds.

Table 5: Blue Bonds Initiatives

Bond	Objective	Size and Duration	Investors	Key Terms
Seychelles Blue Bond (October 2018)	Transition support to sustainable fisheries	$15 million; 10 years	World Bank; Private Placement: Calvert Impact Capital; Nuveen, and Prudential	Loan provided by GEF reduced interest rate for government from 6.5% to 2.8%
Nordic–Baltic Blue Bond (January 2019)	Bond issuances focus on investments within water resource management and protection	$213 million; 5 years	Capital Market	3.75% coupon
Morgan Stanley and the World Bank (April 2019)	Sustainable Development Bond to draw attention to the challenge of plastic waste pollution in ocean	$10 million; 3 years	Capital Market	Callable step-up fixed rate bond Year 1: 2.35% Year 2: 2.70% Year 3: 3.15%

continued on next page

Table 5 continued

Bond	Objective	Size and Duration	Investors	Key Terms
Bank of China (September 2020)	Finance marine-related green projects across various domestic and overseas markets.	$ 942.5 million equivalent	Banks and other financial institutions, asset managers, private banks, and insurance companies and other investors.	**Tranche 1:** $500 million bond priced at 99.694% with a coupon of 0.950% to offer a yield of 1.054% (~ 90 bps above US treasury) **Tranche 2:** $442.5 million, priced at par with similar coupon and reoffer yield of 3.15%
ADB Blue Bond (September 2021)	The proceeds will finance projects that enhance ocean health through ecosystem restoration, natural resources management, sustainable fisheries and aquaculture, reduction of coastal pollution, circular economy, marine renewable energy, and green ports and shipping.	Dual-tranche: a. $150 million; 15 years b. $150 million; 10 years	a. The Dai-chi Life Insurance Company b. Meiji Yasuda Life Insurance Company	a. AUD208 million Coupon: 1.8% Tenor: 15 years b. NZD217 million Coupon: 2.1525% Tenor: 10 years

ASEAN = Association of Southeast Asian Nations, GEF = Global Environment Facility, US = United States.
Source: The ASEAN Catalytic Green Finance Facility.

f. Blue Carbon Credits

Blue carbon refers to the carbon stored in "coastal and marine ecosystems." Those ecosystems include mangroves forests, tidal marshes, and seagrass beds. Those ocean and coastal habitats circulate 83% of the world's carbon and have the ability to store a significant amount of CO_2. Many organizations, such as The Blue Carbon Initiative, are working to restore, protect, and grow the coastal areas that house blue carbon and keep emissions away from the atmosphere (Box 11). The carbon-capturing companies or municipalities can also sell those credits to the businesses that are emitting carbon for a profit. Many financial companies and industrial emitters are currently purchasing carbon offsets for future compliance.[89] The Blue Carbon Resilience Credit (BCRC) markets could mobilize as much as $320 million per year for coastal conservation and restoration projects.[90] The blue carbon concept is still being developed, with initial support from philanthropy and corporate social responsibility funds, and yet to be mainstreamed as a large scale market opportunity. Some of the projects being considered for adopting the blue carbon mode include offshore seagrass farming, that can sell blue carbon credits, while having a revenue stream from the sale of seagrass itself.[91]

---

[89] Tierra Resources. Frequently Asked Questions.
[90] Climate Finance Lab. Blue Carbon Resilience Credit.
[91] Oceans 2050.

Box 11: The Kaimana Conservation Initiative in Indonesia

The Kaimana Conservation Initiative based in Indonesia was able to access carbon-based funding for sustainable use and conservation activities. Indonesia is home to 20% of the world's mangroves and has the largest annual climate mitigation potential of any one country in the world. Almost 30 million tons of emissions could be reduced from avoided mangrove conversion in Indonesia. The country's mangroves are being lost at a rate of up to 2% per year however, mainly due to deforestation for aquaculture and agriculture.

Source: The Blue Carbon Initiative. Kaimana Coastal Conservation and Community Development – Indonesia.

There are a number of other instruments such as sustainability linked loans, revolving loan funds, transition bonds, and transition finance that are being considered for the blue economy projects. Each of the instruments are being contextualized for the specific project or the geography as the case may be. The diversity of the initiatives indicate the efforts that are being made, while also point to the lack of standardized and universally accepted mainstreamed options at this current stage, which addresses the underlying characteristics of the blue economy projects.

4 OCEAN HEALTH CREDIT FINANCE MECHANISM: A PROPOSED ACCELERATOR

Bountiful catch. A net full of freshly caught fish in Gentuma Raya, Gontalo, Indonesia (photo by Eric Sales/ADB).

"There is a need for structuring and creating bankable blue economy projects, as many of them do not have appropriate risk-return profiles as required by commercial investors."

RAMESH SUBRAMANIAM, DIRECTOR GENERAL, SOUTHEAST ASIA DEPARTMENT, ADB

Interventions relating to policy, governance, regulation, infrastructure improvement, technology, operating practices, and fiscal instruments are expected to ensure sustainability of the blue economy. The objective is to mitigate the further damage to the water bodies and turn toward more sustainable living. If the direct and indirect benefits (relating to health care, livelihoods, education, credit, infrastructure, political participation, etc.) resulting from blue economy interventions could be captured and financially valued, these could potentially become an additionality to the project revenues, as was witnessed in creation of carbon credits and trading of the same.

As the blue economy and financing instruments continue to develop, they provide public and private sector organizations with tools that can bring in the needed investments. However, the blue economy financing market is not without risks and challenges. The lack of widely accepted definitions of what is considered "blue investments" (how proceeds are tracked, managed, and reported on), and the lack of assurance requirements over information reported are substantial constraint.

Blue economy projects will need a combination of grants, concessional finance, and adequate underwriting to be able to achieve financial close. The current reliance on official development assistance and philanthropy needs to be substantially augmented to achieve scale that can have visible impact on improving ocean health. There is a need therefore for a facility (or facilities) that can provide the innovative structuring support to develop, in comparison to conventional development finance instruments, better project models and better financing instruments or products that are specifically targeted to providing desired returns to the users and de-risking of project structures. It must also be able to support multiple projects configured either by the public sector project proponents or private sector developers.

A. Overview

The ocean health mechanism (structured as a facility) is envisaged to provide tailored concessional finance and de-risking instruments to blue economy projects along with support for structuring sustainable project models and improving institutional capacity. The objectives of the ocean health mechanism include:

(i)   assistance in structuring blue economy projects to increase their bankability;
(ii)   attracting public, private, and philanthropic sources of capital to ocean growth projects, where it would not otherwise flow; and
(iii)   supporting achievement of the SDGs through:

- infrastructure creation;
- redevelopment and maintenance; and
- policy and enforcement.

The touchstone principles behind the mechanism include:

(i) configuring a country or region-specific "ocean health mechanism" such that projects integrate infrastructure development, sustainable human economic activities with clear indicators for improving ocean health and sustainable livelihoods, for instance linked to the ADB Ocean Finance Framework principles, country SDG commitments, and/or nationally determined contributions;

(ii) improving capacities of national and local governments and help them in developing a pipeline of well prepared and high impact "blue finance" projects;

(iii) creating or identifying a dedicated public sector agency or facility with contributions from governments, multilateral and bilateral agencies like ADB, commercial investors and institutions, impact investors, philanthropists, and other project stakeholders;

(iv) defining principles for use of this fund explicitly or adopt existing principles such as ADB Ocean Finance Framework and bankability criteria, as a leveraging or de-risking fund which can support blue finance projects to become bankable, affordable to end users;

(v) supporting development of blue finance instruments and mechanisms at state-owned entities, local and regional governments; and

(vi) ensuring rapid implementation and clear monitoring of projects to ensure that climate change targets are being met, and timely release of impact data to the investment community (with an agreed set of metrics developed and adopted for impact reporting).

The contours of the proposed mechanism is presented in Figure 8.

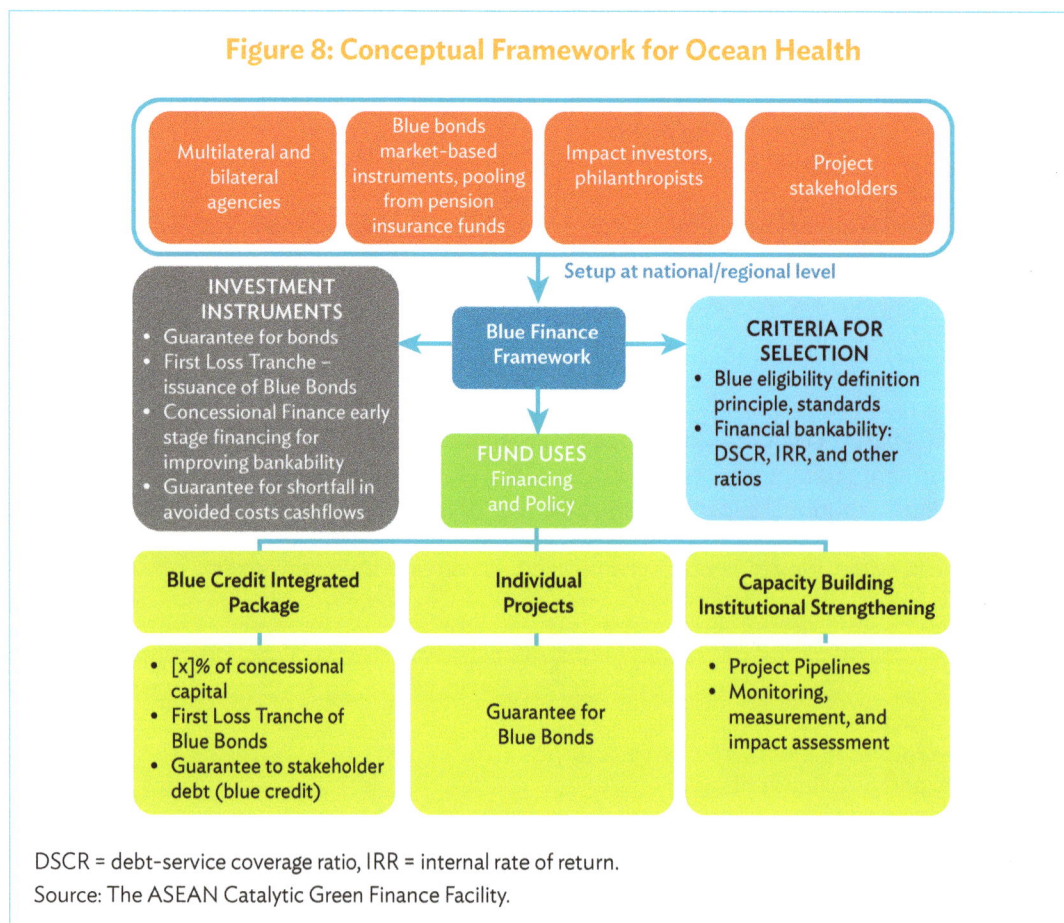

Figure 8: Conceptual Framework for Ocean Health

DSCR = debt-service coverage ratio, IRR = internal rate of return.
Source: The ASEAN Catalytic Green Finance Facility.

B. Structure and Governance

The ocean health mechanism, to be set up either at a regional or national level, will identify, originate, design, and structure projects based on blue eligibility principles and standards agreed upon, along with an objective to achieve desired financial bankability metrics. As there are no universally agreed metrics or eligibility criteria, a set of principles could be agreed upon based on frameworks such as the ADB Ocean Finance Framework or developed for the extant context. The governance structure of the ocean health mechanism could comprise independent sector advisors in addition to the executive and investment support teams to provide a comprehensive oversight toward achieving the sustainability objectives.

1. Sources of Funds

The ocean health mechanism would need to have the potential to offer concessional finance, technical assistance support, and credit enhancements or guarantees. The capital structure of the facility could be a mixture of grant funds, zero interest loans, and concessional funds. It would draw its sources of funds through a combination of

(i) government budgetary allocations (including those committed in climate change nationally determined contributions [NDCs] and SDGs);

(ii) multilateral and bilateral agencies and development partners;

(iii) pension, insurance funds, and debt funds;

(iv) impact investors, including foundations, family offices, high net worth individuals, with strongly aligned mandates;

(v) philanthropists;

(vi) contributions toward corporate social responsibility; and

(vii) project stakeholders including affected parties, beneficiaries and economic generating units.

2. Investment Criteria and Instruments

The supported initiatives by the ocean health mechanism would need to meet the blue project eligibility, and the project financials need to be bankable. The blue project eligibility ascertains if the projects adhere to any of the accepted guidelines that define blue economy such as those being developed by ADB. These projects could typically span across the land and ocean. The projects could have metrics that estimate the potential benefits, which would be verified and monitored. The financial bankability could be assessed as meeting a target debt service coverage ratio (e.g., a minimum of 1.05 every year with a minimum average debt service coverage ratio of 1.50 over the loan life).

The ocean health mechanism would provide flexibility to use the available funds in a manner that best meets the requirements of the project or initiative under consideration. The funds could be used to provide capital and/or operational support for a period through various instruments such as:

(i) concessional finance, which is early-stage financing for improving bankability;

(ii) first loss tranche, the issuance of blue bonds; and

(iii) guarantee ("ocean health credit guarantee") for blue bond repayments and shortfall in cash flows arising from avoided costs.

The ocean health mechanism would integrate with the traditional project risk insurance products and would be suitably structured to reflect regional requirements (e.g., disbursement in local currency, hedging, and insurance requirements).

3. Deployment of Funds

The funds could be used to support

(i) specific government-originated projects (through an integrated package comprising project development, structuring, and financing components using a variety of investment instruments) that have limited revenue streams, but have considerable potential for avoided costs and environmental savings;

(ii) individual projects promoted by private investors and/or project developers that adhere to the blue principles; and

(iii) knowledge, awareness, and capacity building for institutional development and pipeline creation.

a. Public Sector Projects

It is expected that a significant component of the ocean health mechanism would be used to catalyze high impact nature positive projects, which the public sector project proponents will be mandated to develop and implement. These could typically be environment- or livelihood-focused projects with significantly lower revenue streams (and hence, with not easily amenable for commercial financing), but those having considerable environment, ecological, and social returns. Table 6 presents a list of potential projects.

Table 6: Potential Blue Economy Projects

Category	Sector	Projects
Ocean-based	• fisheries, aquaculture, food security • ecotourism or sustainable tourism, MPAs	• Sustainable fisheries, cold storage, logistics, seafood processing, integrated fisheries management. • Management and restoration of critical marine ecosystems, including through marine protected areas and nature-based solutions. • Resorts or lodging, recreational facilities, protected areas for tourist destinations. • PPP for co-management of MPAs. • Offshore and floating solar. • Other marine renewables. • Aquaculture, mariculture, algaculture, alternative feeds, reduced pollution, reduced dependency on wild-caught fish.
Land-based	• pollution reduction and waste management • water use and supply management • coastal transport • energy: marine and renewable • enterprise and livelihood development	• Domestic and industrial wastewater treatment. • Management of hazardous and nonhazardous wastes from domestic, industrial, commercial, and institutional sources. • Management of runoff from agricultural land or operations. • Integrated surface and groundwater management. • Management of water resources and ground water recharge. • Greening of ports and decarbonization of shipping.

continued on next page

Table 6 *continued*

Category	Sector	Projects
Others	• habitat protection, restoration, and management • natural and manmade hazard prevention and management • integrated coastal development and implementation • oil and gas • sustainable seabed mining	• Wetlands management and restoration. • Infrastructure resilience improvements. • Disaster preparedness and response facilities and services. • Oil spill response. • Marine biotechnology. • Environmental monitoring, reporting, and information management. • Capacity building.

ASEAN = Association of Southeast Asian Nations, MPA = marine protected area, PPP = public–private partnership.
Source: The ASEAN Catalytic Green Finance Facility.

The ocean health mechanism can provide an integrated package of funding for such projects comprising institutional capacity building support, project financing, and credit enhancement support. The capacity building support could be in the form of assistance in generating and developing project pipelines, preliminary project structuring, monitoring, measurement and impact assessment, institutional strengthening of project sponsors, policy, governance and institutional strengthening, and knowledge dissemination.

The instruments that could potentially be part of the ocean health mechanism include concessional finance, guarantee for bonds and revenue support structures, and subscription to first loss tranches. The ocean health mechanism aims to support projects that need concessional finance in the early stages of project development, construction, and operations to accelerate their implementation. The project financing support could primarily be a senior debt at concessional rates (e.g., 20% to 40% of project cost at 0.75% for 25 years). It is expected that the government would contribute to the project, also drawing from the resources available to meet the climate change commitments (nationally determined contributions).

The mechanism would provide support to catalyze investments from other sources including private or commercial investors, impact investors, and project stakeholders (those who are directly or indirectly affected by the project, or those who have affinity to the sector or region). The indicative components of a financing plan could be as follows:

- facility: [20%–40%] of capex debt at [0.75%] for [10–25] years;
- government contribution;
- private or commercial investors;
- if PPP, then private equity and capital; and
- impact investors and project stakeholders through mechanisms such as bonds, where feasible.

In addition to providing the senior debt, the ocean health mechanism would provide an underwriting for bonds, if raised for the project. The ocean health mechanism would guarantee ([x%] of the principal amounts raised as "blue" bonds and interest thereon). The cost of the guarantee would be charged to the project nominally. To encourage mezzanine financing, the mechanism could guarantee the shortfall of the revenue cash flow streams from that of the projected ones.

Given the nature of projects that are likely to be developed by the public sector proponents (those with very limited revenue streams or less potential to meet the project costs), the ocean health mechanism could assist the proponents in developing innovative finance instruments. One such instruments could be an "ocean health credit." This ocean health credit could be configured either as a certificate or structured note or as predetermined payments to the project for achieving desired impacts.

Option I: Certificate or Structured Note

The impact investors or project stakeholders could issue "ocean health credits," an instrument (certificate or structured note) that offers a rate of return in line with other similar environmental, social, and governance (ESG) products when held to maturity. The tenor could be a long term (e.g., 10–15 years). The returns on the ocean health credit could be structured with minimal payments in the initial years (so as to provide immediate low-cost funds to the project proponents), with rates stepping up over a period. The investors could have the option to either hold on until maturity and exit (with returns similar to other ESG instruments) or can be given an option to convert their investment into equity. The timing of such exit or conversion to equity could be at predetermined points in time, for instance, once after completion of construction and stabilized operations or second at the end of the tenor of the instrument. The conversion into equity would provide these investors a stake in the project and increased community participation. The guarantee component of the blue finance framework would be extended to the (full) principal and interest for the ocean health credit investors at the time of exit.

The cashflow available for debt service of the blue economy projects could be generated through a combination of project revenues, project sponsor's contributions from buoyancy in local taxes, and/or revenues. In addition, the project could consider capturing the value of "avoided costs" and use the same as an additionality.

The avoided costs, for the purposes of this context, refer to those incremental capital, operating and social expenses that would have to be spent if the project did not proceed. In effect, they are the savings realized by the project sponsor (on the business-as-usual scenario without the project) over a period of time. Depending on the sector, these avoided costs could relate to savings in salaries, repairs, maintenance, insurance premiums, health system costs, area being used for landfills, treatment facilities, or in direct pay-outs to those elements that impact the environment (beach maintenance, governance and compliance etc.). For example, investments in wastewater treatment can lead to cleaner coastal water bodies, which improve the health of local populations who swim in them and eat fish, thereby reducing health costs. The quantification of such avoided costs could be based on the principles of economic appraisal (based on the incremental costs and benefits and involves comparison of project costs and benefits under the "with" and "without" project scenario) and securitization of future cash flows.

The mechanics of assessing the avoided costs could be as follows:

- The project proponent and one potential investor or lender (with the support of an independent entity) assess the current costs incurred, which have the potential to decrease if the project were to be implemented, including the pay-outs (on elements such as health care, livelihoods, education, credit, infrastructure, political participation, etc.) (business- as-usual scenario).

- Configure a project (intervention such as an MPA or a river rejuvenation), including the capital, operations and maintenance costs, and any conventional revenue streams (user charges, etc.).

- Estimate the reduction in the costs from the business-as-usual scenario (avoided costs). These costs would be ringfenced and made available as part of the project cash flows along with other potential revenue streams. Any shortfall on the estimated cashflows from this "avoided costs" could be guaranteed by the ocean health mechanism, subject to covenants on diligence and integrity.

- Formulate an overall cash flow for the project (incorporating the avoided costs).

- The investor or lender assesses the future cash flows and provides funds against the same as project equity or debt (or any hybrid structure). The contributions from the impact investors or the local project stakeholders could be made against the issuance of ocean health credits.

- The ocean health mechanism would operate with a covenant that the government acts against the polluters by imposing fines or penalties, which will be transferred to the project revenues.

- Other sources of cash flows could also be structured for suitable projects. The polluters could buy the ocean health credits and are entitled to continue their business for a predetermined period (similar to the functioning in carbon credits market), subject to a long-term commitment to contain their activities. The proceeds from such purchases will be used to finance the project under consideration.

This mechanism could potentially provide an opportunity for large-scale participation of the stakeholders (impact investors and local stakeholders), with the blue finance framework providing an assurance of returns on investment.

Option II: Predetermined Payments

This would essentially entail the national entity or sovereign (through the blue finance framework) providing a predetermined annual payment or ocean health credits to a project implementing entity linked to performance or impact indicators that a project needs to achieve, such as those set out in ADB Ocean Finance Framework (e.g., reduction in pollution load levels, share of area under no-take management, fish biomass, etc.).

The main aim would be to support the public project proponents to finance most of the capital expenditure through the financing sources available including leveraging public and/or development financing assistance with commercial capital. The project proponents would need to take the construction risk and subsequently focus on operational efficiencies, while insulated from revenue risks as long as project benefits are delivered. The revenue additionality would be provided from the ocean health credits. The mechanism of ocean health credits should be seen as aligned with the principle of avoided costs from alleviating future economic or health disasters, such as diseases arising from lack of access to clean water, polluted river bodies or decline in fishing stocks. An estimate of such avoided costs could provide a benchmark to limit the level of ocean health credits provided to a project.

The need for this financial support will likely fade over time once scale and technologies improve, costs are reduced, and sustainability is achieved. The financial sustainability of blue economy projects is expected to improve when the sector develops, governments create conducive regulatory environments and financial incentives, and counterproductive subsidies are eliminated. The payment mechanism for such ocean health credits could be ringfenced into the blue finance framework funded by governments, multilateral development banks, and donors.

b. Private Initiated Projects

The ocean health mechanism would support "blue economy" projects initiated by private sponsors, which have untested revenue streams, or those adopting new technologies or those with significant blue economy benefits. The facility would offer guarantee ("ocean health credit guarantee" at concessional rates) on debt repayment to the blue bond holders for a defined percentage of the principal and interest payments. The extent of support could be based on the project, geography, and the project proponent characteristics.

c. Capacity Building and Institutional Strengthening

Creating the impact desired by various initiatives of governments and other stakeholders concerned would depend on generating a continuous pipeline of projects that are ready for investment. There is a substantial need to improve the knowledge and awareness, particularly among the public sector stakeholders, about the sector as a whole, project configurations, possible financing modalities, and implementation through various public and private sector arrangements. There is also a need to support the monitoring, measurement, and impact assessment activities that need to be undertaken for the blue economy projects. The ocean health mechanism can assist in financing these activities.

5 POTENTIAL INITIATIVES IN SOUTHEAST ASIA

Tourism development. The upgraded road allowed tourists to get to Honda Bay in less time, thus quadrupling the number of arrivals to 40,000 per year. The increase benefited fishing families who also provide tourist services like island-hopping and ecotourism tours (photo by Ariel Javellana/ADB).

Different countries are configuring their plans to achieve their NDCs through a range of technical, institutional, policy, governance, and advocacy measures. Financing the initiatives is gaining more prominence, as witnessed in the increasing number of commitments from the public and private sectors and civil society. Most Southeast Asian countries have listed improvement in the marine and fisheries sectors as one of their primary actions. There has been an explicit interest for private capital in supporting reforms in fisheries management, together with substantial community engagement. Indonesia and Cambodia, for instance, have been contemplating developing facilities that promote sustainable fisheries along with associated infrastructure.

A. Indonesia

The National Development Planning Agency (BAPPENAS) of Indonesia intends to develop a Marine and Fisheries Financing Institution (MFFI), potentially to be housed within PT Sarana Multi Infrastruktur (Persero) (PT SMI). This institution is being developed in association with Rare and ADB. This subnational vehicle is an innovative financing structure that enables commercial capital to be catalyzed and filtered to local governments, with the purpose of optimizing the financing and delivery of sustainable coastal fisheries management, marine conservation, and associated infrastructure. The structure envisages to harness the limited capital pool from public and philanthropic sources to optimize the risk–return profile of its investable natural resource assets and reduce the perceived risks. The MFFI intends to use various blended financial instruments such as first loss capital and guarantees to incentivize private investors.

The MFFI will ensure, through a rigorous process of project selection, implementation guidelines, and criteria, reporting on the use of proceeds, that loans provided to local governments are used for purposes that are aligned with its mandate. Local governments that borrow from the MFFI will be required to report on the use of the funds according to stringent criteria showing impact and outputs as detailed in project proposals. This will enhance the ability of local governments to borrow and create a municipal bond market, in line with Indonesia's success in the green bond market (Box 12) .

Box 12: Indonesia's Success with Green Bonds

Indonesia's lead in the green bond market makes it well-poised to upscale investments in the blue economy. Indonesia has the second largest green bond market among member states of the Association of Southeast Asian Nations, with 24% of total regional issuance. Singapore remained the regional leader on green bond issuance, with 53% of the $9.3 billion issued in Southeast Asia, and the Philippines and Thailand follow with 9% and 8% respectively.

The Government of Indonesia issued the world's first sovereign green sukuk in 2018. The deal was hugely oversubscribed and had to be upsized to $1.25 billion priced at 3.75%. HSBC acted as green structuring advisor. Abu Dhabi Islamic Bank, Bank CIMB Niaga, Citigroup, Dubai Islamic Bank, and HSBC were joint bookrunners.

The proceeds raised from the placement will go to multiple projects from eligible categories such as renewable energy, public transport, low-carbon buildings, water and waste management, and green tourism.

Alignment of Indonesia's low-carbon and climate-resilient infrastructure with international definitions of "green" can help attract private overseas capital.

a Sukuk is a sharia-compliant bond-like instrument used in Islamic finance.
Source: Climate Bonds Initiative. 2018. Green Infrastructure Investment Opportunities Indonesia; Climate Bonds Initiative. 2021. ASEAN Sustainable Finance State of the Market 2020. April.

B. Cambodia

Cambodia's fisheries sector contributes almost 6% of the national GDP over a quarter of the agricultural GDP. As Cambodia progresses toward middle-income status, the fisheries sector is focusing on transformation. Constraints to the coastal and marine fisheries include (i) poor and unhygienic condition of post-harvest physical infrastructure, (ii) limited value addition to fish and fishery products, (iii) limited access to finance for smallholders and small and medium-sized entrepreneurs, and (iv) degradation of coastal and marine ecosystems due unsustainable practices. The Fisheries Administration of the Ministry of Agriculture, Forestry and Fisheries has recognized the importance of developing the entire value chain for achieving better markets for Cambodia's marine fisheries resources, and to deliver higher quality and unique products. Cambodia's Strategic Planning Framework for Fisheries (2015–2024) has clear goals and objectives for inclusive development of the sector to contribute to national economy and food security, while the Tourism Development Strategic Plan 2012–2020 provides a framework for planning and indicates the Government of Cambodia's desire for sustainable tourism development, including sustainable management of coastal zone ecosystems as tourism assets. Investment in sustainable management of marine fisheries provides an opportunity for development of the blue economy while at the same time enhancing the value of coastal and marine ecosystems increased fisheries productivity and its tourism assets.

As part of the Sustainable Coastal and Marine Fisheries Project, it is envisaged to create a blue financing structure that would assist in developing projects including (i) modular renewably powered cold storage and ice-making; (ii) digitization of seafood production and use of smart phone apps to provide direct to market sale of seafood; (iii) advanced open water aquaculture including controlled environment systems (e.g., giant fish cages) and other systems; (iv) possible generation of a large volume of "blue" carbon credits (which may deliver a dividend to the overall investment operation); (v) PPP for open water aquaculture (cross-sector collaboration); (vi) establishment of mangroves and artificial reefs for coastal resilience; and (vii) cleaner boats (e.g., electric, hybrid, and fuel cell propulsion systems, may be deployed on a pilot basis, or retrofitting of existing boats). The financing structure would also assist in developing a range of policy and institutional strengthening initiatives.[92]

These initiatives by the Governments of Indonesia and Cambodia provide examples of how the financing landscape in Southeast Asia is rapidly changing while demonstrating the need to engage with a variety of stakeholders. The financing mechanism envisaged illustrates the requirement to configure a facility that comprehensively addresses the challenges of ocean health, livelihoods, food security, and economic activities. The ADB is proactively working with countries in the region in developing further the proposed facility so the economies that are most impacted by ocean pollution, such as Indonesia, the Philippines, Thailand, and Viet Nam, can benefit from initiatives that span across project development, access to finance and capacity to participate in blue economy projects

---

[92] ADB. Cambodia: Sustainable Coastal and Marine Fisheries Project.

6 CONCLUSION

Community effort: Neighbors helping each other pull a fishing net in Gentuma Raya, Gorontalo, Indonesia (photo by Eric Sales/ADB).

For a flourishing blue economy, a range of financing sources including private sector investment is imperative. However, private sector will not participate without clarity on the returns and some sense of the wider opportunity to make money sustainably in and from the ocean. Public institutions can help bridge this gap. By designing policy mechanisms to allow new and sustainable marine activities to succeed, governments can help populate a pipeline of projects for willing investors. Between these different roles and activities, a well-defined framework is needed to allow for high-level coordination between the public and private sectors to unlock blue economy investment. A blue finance mechanism will establish project selections criteria and guide the measurement of impact to allow finance to be incentivizing the best projects.

The blue finance mechanism aims to assist in undertaking policy and governance related initiatives to curb pollution and to accelerate the investments into the ocean sector with adoption of innovative financial instruments such as ocean health credits. Through such regional facility, it is anticipated that partnerships among diverse stakeholders including government, NGOs, and private, financial, monitoring and evaluation, research, and academic agencies be fostered. Such partnerships could mainstream impact investment in the blue economy, generate project pipelines, and offer opportunities to pool resources with newer structures.

References

Ahmed, M. 2019. Blue Bonds: What They Are, and How They Can Help the Oceans. *World Economic Forum.* 6 June. https://www.weforum.org/agenda/2019/06/world-oceans-day-blue-bonds-can-help-guarantee-the-oceans-wealth/.

Althelia Funds. https://althelia.com/sustainable-ocean-fund/.

ASEAN Centre for Biodiversity. https://aseanbiodiversity.org/.

Asian Development Bank (ADB). 2017. *Meeting Asia's Infrastructure Needs.* Manila. https://doi.org/10.22617/FLS168388-2.

———. 2019. ADB Launches $5 Billion Healthy Oceans Action Plan. 2 May. https://www.adb.org/news/adb-launches-5-billion-healthy-oceans-action-plan.

———. 2021. ADB Issues First Blue Bond for Ocean Investments. 10 September. https://www.adb.org/news/adb-issues-first-blue-bond-ocean-investments.

———. 2021. ADB Blue Bonds. September. https://www.adb.org/publications/adb-blue-bonds.

———. Overview: ASEAN Catalytic Green Finance Facility (ACGF). https://www.adb.org/what-we-do/funds/asean-catalytic-green-finance-facility/overview.

———. Regional: Fourth Greater Mekong Subregion Corridor Towns Development Project. https://www.adb.org/projects/50099-001/main.

———. Cambodia: Sustainable Coastal and Marine Fisheries Project. https://www.adb.org/projects/53261-001/main.

ADB, Coral Triangle Initiative, and Global Environment Facility. 2014. *Regional State of the Coral Triangle—Coral Triangle Marine Resources: Their Status, Economies, and Management.* https://www.adb.org/publications/regional-state-coral-triangle-marine-resources-their-status-economies-and-management.

Association of Southeast Asian Nations (ASEAN). 2012. ASEAN Sectoral Integration Protocol for Fisheries. 11 May. https://asean.org/?static_post=asean-sectoral- integration-protocol-for-fisheries.

———. ASEAN Cooperation on Coastal and Marine Environment. https://environment.asean.org/awgcme/.

Bariletti, M. 2019. Credit Enhancement: A Boost to Private Capital in Infrastructure? World Bank Blogs. 17 January. https://blogs.worldbank.org/ppps/credit-enhancement-boost-private-capital-infrastructure.

Becatoros, E. 2017. More than 90 Percent of World's Coral Reefs Will Die by 2050. *The Independent.* 13 March. https://www.independent.co.uk/climate-change/news/environment-90-percent-coral-reefs-die-2050-climate-change-bleaching-pollution-a7626911.html.

Blue Carbon Initiative. 2019. Kaimana Coastal Conservation and Community Development—Indonesia. https://www.thebluecarboninitiative.org/blue-carbon-activities/2019/4/26/kaimana-coastal-conservation-and-community-development-indonesia.

Blue Finance. http://blue-finance.org.

Blue Natural Capital Financing Facility. https://bluenaturalcapital.org/.

Borrelle, S. B. et al. 2020. Predicted Growth in Plastic Waste Exceeds Efforts to Mitigate Plastic Pollution. *Science*. 369 (6509). pp. 1515–1518. https://doi.org/10.1126/SCIENCE.ABA3656.

Brookings Institute, Global Economy and Development at Brookings. 2017. G20 Brainstorming Workshop: Mobilizing Private Finance for Sustainable Infrastructure. Buenos Aires, Argentina. 7–8 September. https://www.brookings.edu/wp-content/uploads/2017/11/mobilizing-private-finance-for-sustainable-infrastructure-brief.pdf.

Caribbean Development Bank. 2018. Financing the Blue Economy: A Caribbean Development Opportunity. 31 May. https://www.caribank.org/publications-and-resources/resource-library/thematic-papers/financing-blue-economy-caribbean-development-opportunity.

Circulate Capital. 2019. *Investing to Reduce Plastic Pollution in South and Southeast Asia: A Handbook for Action*. https://oursharedseas.com/oss_downloads/investing-to-reduce-plastic-pollution-in-south-and-southeast-asia-a-handbook-for-action/.

Climate Bonds Initiative. 2018. *Green Infrastructure Investment Opportunities Indonesia*. https://www.climatebonds.net/resources/reports/green-infrastructure-investment-opportunities-indonesia.

—————. 2021. Sustainable Debt: Global State of the Market 2020. April. https://www.climatebonds.net/resources/reports/sustainable-debt-global-state-market-2020.

Climate Finance Lab. Blue Carbon Resilience Credit. https://www.climatefinancelab.org/project/blue-carbon-resilience-credit/.

Clouse, C. J. 2019. With Oceans in Peril, Investors Find New Ways to Invest in the "Blue Economy." *Impact Alpha*. 28 March. https://impactalpha.com/with-oceans-in-peril-investors-find-new-ways-to-invest-in-the-blue-economy/.

Coalition for Private Investment in Conservation. http://cpicfinance.com/.

Colgan, C. S. 2003. Measurement of the Ocean and Coastal Economy: Theory and Methods. *Publications*. Paper 3. National Ocean Economics Program. 1 December. https://citeseerx.ist.psu.edu/viewdoc/download?doi=10.1.1.673.1640&rep=rep1&type=pdf.

Costello, C. et al. 2020. The Future of Food from the Sea. *Nature*. 588. pp. 95–100. 19 August. https://doi.org/10.1038/s41586-020-2616-y.

Credit Suisse and WWF. 2014. *Conservation Finance: Moving Beyond Donor Funding Toward an Investor-Driven Approach*. https://earthmind.org/sites/default/files/2014-ConservationFinanceMovingBeyondDonorFundinglnvestorDrivenApproach.pdf.

Cunningham, W. P. and M. A. Cunningham. 2016. *Principles of Environmental Science: Inquiry and Application.* McGraw Hill.

Development Asia. 2020. The Role of Ocean Finance in Transitioning to a Blue Economy in Asia and the Pacific. 8 June. https://development.asia/explainer/role-ocean-finance-transitioning-blue-economy-asia-and-pacific.

Díaz, S. et al., eds. 2019. *Summary for Policymakers of the IPBES Global Assessment Report on Biodiversity and Ecosystem Services.* Intergovernmental Science-Policy Platform on Biodiversity and Ecosystem Services (IPBES). https://www.ipbes.net/document-library-catalogue/summary-policymakers-global-assessment-laid-out.

Earthworks. 2019. Dumping by the Numbers. https://www.earthworks.org/cms/assets/uploads/2018/02/DOD-FactSheet-DumpingByNumbers-012919-3.pdf.

Environmental Defense Fund. 2018. Environmental Impact Bonds: Financing for Wetlands Restoration. https://www.edf.org/ecosystems/environmental-impact-bonds-financing-wetlands-restoration.

Environmental Defense Fund, Rare/Meloy Fund, and Encourage Capital. 2018. Principles for Investment in Sustainable Wild-Caught Fisheries. http://www.fisheriesprinciples.org/files/2019/05/updated-PrinciplesInvestmentWEB_final.pdf.

European Commission. 2012. Blue Growth Opportunities for Marine and Maritime Sustainable Growth. https://www.unep.org/resources/report/blue-growth-opportunities-marine-and-maritime-sustainable-growth.

European Commission. 2017. Report on the Blue Growth Strategy Towards More Sustainable Growth and Jobs in the Blue Economy. 31 March. http://www.bluemed-project.eu/wp-content/uploads/2017/05/Annex-VI-SWD2017128-final-Blue-Growth-.pdf.

European Commission, WWF, HRH the Prince of Wales' International Sustainability Unit, and European Investment Bank. 2017. Introducing the Sustainable Blue Economy Finance Principles. https://www.investableoceans.com/blogs/insights/introducing-the-sustainable-blue-economy-finance-principles.

European Commission. Reducing Emissions from the Shipping Sector. https://ec.europa.eu/clima/policies/transport/shipping_en.

European Parliament, Library. 2013. Blue Growth Sustainable Development of EU Marine and Coastal Sectors. Library Briefing. 6 May. https://www.europarl.europa.eu/RegData/bibliotheque/briefing/2013/130522/LDM_BRI(2013)130522_REV1_EN.pdf.

Food and Agriculture Organization of the United Nations (FAO). 2014. The State of World Fisheries and Aquaculture: Opportunities and Challenges. Rome. http://www.fao.org/3/i3720e/i3720e.pdf.

FAO. 2018. Pollutants from Agriculture a Serious Threat to World's Water. 20 June. http://www.fao.org/news/story/en/item/1141534/icode/.

Fourth Ministerial Forum on the Sustainable Development Strategy for the Seas of East Asia. 2012. Changwon Declaration Toward an Ocean Based Blue Economy: Moving Ahead with the Sustainable Development Strategy. Changwon, Republic of Korea. 12 July. http://pemsea.org/sites/default/files/changwon-declaration_0.pdf.

Global Environment Facility, United Nations Development Programme, and Partnerships in Environmental Management for the Seas of East Asia (PEMSEA). 2018. *Blue Economy Growth in the East Asian Seas Region*. http://pemsea.org/sites/default/files/Regional_SOC_20190611.pdf.

Global Water Partnership. 2017. Pollution Charges. https://www.gwp.org/en/learn/iwrm-toolbox/Management-Instruments/Economic-Instruments/Pollution_charges/.

Government of the United States, Department of Commerce, National Oceanic and Atmospheric Administration, National Ocean Service. How Much Oxygen Comes from the Ocean? https://oceanservice.noaa.gov/facts/ocean-oxygen.html.

Government of the United States, Environmental Protection Agency, Water Infrastructure and Resiliency Finance Center. 2017. *DC Water's Environmental Impact Bond: A First of its Kind*. April. https://www.epa.gov/sites/production/files/2017-04/documents/dc_waters_environmental_impact_bond_a_first_of_its_kind_final2.pdf.

Guggisberg, S. 2018. Funding Coastal and Marine Fisheries Projects under the Climate Change Regime. *Marine Policy*. 107. September. https://doi.org/10.1016/j.marpol.2018.11.015.

Hoegh-Guldberg, O. et al. 2015. Reviving the Ocean Economy: The Case for Action 2015. Geneva: WWF International. https://wwfint.awsassets.panda.org/downloads/reviving_ocean_economy_report_hi_res.pdf.

Hooper, K. 2017. Diving into Sustainable Marine Protected Area Management in the Philippines. Solutions. 1 March. https://thesolutionsjournal.com/2017/03/01/diving-sustainable-marine-protected-area-management-philippines/.

Joint World Health Organization (WHO)/Food and Agriculture Organization of the United Nations (FAO) Consultation on Diet, Nutrition and the Prevention of Chronic Diseases. 2002. Global and Regional Food Consumption Patterns and Trends. Availability and Consumption of Fish. In Diet, Nutrition and the Prevention of Chronic Diseases: Report of a Joint WHO/FAO Expert Consultation. WHO Technical Report Series 916. Geneva. https://www.who.int/dietphysicalactivity/publications/trs916/en/gsfao_global.pdf.

Kaza, S. et al. 2018. *What a Waste 2.0: A Global Snapshot of Solid Waste Management to 2050*. Washington, DC: World Bank. https://doi.org/10.1596/978-1-4648-1329-0.

Konar, M. and H. Ding. 2020. A Sustainable Ocean Economy for 2050: Approximating its Benefits and Costs. High Level Panel for a Sustainable Ocean Economy. https://oceanpanel.org/sites/default/files/2020-07/Ocean Panel_Economic Analysis_FINAL.pdf.

Lebreton, L. C. M. et al. 2017. River Plastic Emissions to the World's Oceans. *Nature Communications*. 8 (15611). 7 June. https://doi.org/10.1038/ncomms15611.

Lindsey, R. 2021. Climate Change: Global Sea Level. *Climate.Gov*. 25 January. https://www.climate.gov/news-features/understanding-climate/climate-change-global-sea-level.

MacFarlane, R. 2019. Marine Litter Problem is Solvable With a Little Help. *Bloomberg Law*. 10 June. https://news. bloombergenvironment.com/environment-and-energy/insight-marine-litter-problem-is-solvable-with-a-little-help.

Markham, A., T. O'Shea, and K. Wachowicz. 2016. *Investing for Sustainable Global Fisheries. Encourage Capital, Bloomberg Philanthropies, and The Rockefeller Foundation*. January. https://www.rockefellerfoundation.org/wp-content/uploads/FULL-REPORT_FINAL_1-11-16.pdf.

Marsh & McLennan Companies. 2017. *Closing the Financing Gap: Infrastructure Project Bankability in Asia.* https://www.marsh.com/sg/insights/research/closing-the-financing-gap-infrastructure-project-bankability-in-asia.html.

Mbaye, S. and M. Badia. 2019. New Data on Global Debt. *International Monetary Fund* (IMF) Blog. 2 January. https://blogs.imf.org/2019/01/02/new-data-on-global-debt/.

McIlgorm, A., H. F. Campbell, and M. J. Rule. 2011. The Economic Cost and Control of Marine Debris Damage in the Asia-Pacific Region. Ocean & Coastal Management. 54 (9). September. pp. 643–651. https://www.sciencedirect.com/science/article/abs/pii/S0964569111000688.

Middlebury Institute of International Studies. Center for the Blue Economy. https://www.middlebury.edu/institute/academics/centers-initiatives/center-blue-economy.

Mirova. 2021. Mirova, IUCN, TASA, Blue Finance and ministry of Blue Economy of Belize announce their partnership in an innovative blended finance facility to improve the management of Belize's marine protected areas & contribute to its blue economy. https://www.mirova.com/en/news/mirova-uicn-tasa-blue-finance-ministry-blue-economy-belize-blended-finance-facility-management-mpas.

Nordic Investment Bank. 2019. NIB Issues first Nordic–Baltic Blue Bond. 24 January. https://www.nib.int/who_we_are/news_and_media/news_press_releases/3170/nib_issues_first_nordic-baltic_blue_bond.

Ocean & Climate Platform. The Ocean, A Carbon Sink. https://ocean-climate.org/en/awareness/the-ocean-a-carbon-sink/.

Ocean Conservancy. 2019. Circulate Capital, U.S. Agency for International Development (USAID), and Ocean Conservancy Announce Blended Finance Partnership to Combat Ocean Plastic Pollution. 5 June. https://oceanconservancy.org/news/circulate-capital-u-s-agency-international-development-usaid-ocean-conservancy-announce-blended-finance-partnership-combat-ocean-plastic-pollution/.

Ocean Conservancy. Plastics in the Ocean. Overview. https://oceanconservancy.org/trash-free-seas/plastics-in-the-ocean/.

Oceana. Shipping Pollution. https://europe.oceana.org/en/shipping-pollution-1.

Oceans 2050. https://www.oceans2050.com/.

Organisation for Economic Co-operation and Development (OECD). 2019. Rethinking Innovation for a Sustainable Ocean Economy. https://www.oecd-ilibrary.org/science-and-technology/rethinking-innovation-for-a-sustainable-ocean-economy_9789264311053-en.

OECD and World Economic Forum (WEF). 2015. Blended Finance Vol. 1: A Primer for Development Finance and Philanthropic Funders. https://assets.ctfassets. net/4cgqlwde6qy0/6hNHDaeN3OOe0m2QgemC2U/9cc4d420b936bb42b5cc7f394bc05579/ World_Economic_Forum__Blended_Finance_Vol._1_-_A_Primer_for_Development_Finance_and_ Philanthropic_Funders__2015.pdf.

OECD and The World Bank. 2016. Climate and Disaster Resilience Financing in Small Island Developing States. 10 November. https://www.oecd-ilibrary.org/development/climate-and-disaster-resilience-financing-in-small-island-developing-states_9789264266919-en.

Ocean Risk and Resilience Action Alliance. https://www.oceanriskalliance.org/.

Office of the Pacific Ocean Commissioner. 2020. Analysis & Development of a Pacific Ocean Bond. *Pacific Ocean Finance Reports*. https://opocbluepacific.net/publications/#64-full-reports.

PEMSEA. 2017. Blue Economy Forum 2017 Proceedings. http://pemsea.org/sites/default/files/Blue Economy Forum 2017 Proceedings (02162018) opt.pdf.

PEMSEA. *Blue Economy*. http://pemsea.org/our-work/blue-economy.

Plastic Soup Foundation. Plastic in Food Chain. https://www.plasticsoupfoundation.org/en/plastic-problem/ plastic-affect-animals/plastic-food-chain/.

Rana, F. 2017. Preparing Bankable Infrastructure Projects. World Bank Blogs. 26 September. https://blogs. worldbank.org/ppps/preparing-bankable-infrastructure-projects.

Ritchie, H. and M. Roser. 2018. Plastic Pollution. *Our World in Data*. https://ourworldindata.org/plastic-pollution#ocean-plastic-sources-land-vs-marine.

Rosembuj, F. and S. Bottio. 2016. Mobilizing Private Climate Finance—Green Bonds and Beyond. EMCompass No. 25. Washington, DC: International Finance Corporation. December. http://documents.worldbank.org/ curated/en/510581481272889882/Mobilizing-private-climate-finance-Green-bonds-and-beyond.

Rowland, M. P. 2017. Two-Thirds of the World's Seafood is Over-fished. *Forbes*. 24 July. https://www.forbes.com/ sites/michaelpellmanrowland/2017/07/24/seafood-sustainability-facts/?sh=6ef2c0ba4bbf.

Regional Plan of Action to Promote Responsible Fishing Practices including Combating IUU Fishing in the Southeast Asia Region. http://www.rpoaiuu.org/.

Ruete, M., M. Aravamuthan, and C. Dominguez. 2015. *Credit Enhancement for Green Projects: Promoting Credit-Enhanced Financing from Multilateral Development Banks for Green Infrastructure Financing*. International Institute for Sustainable Development (IISD). https://www.iisd.org/system/files/publications/credit-enhancement-green-projects.pdf?q=sites/default/files/publications/credit-enhancement-green-projects.pdf/.

Science Daily. 2019. Ocean Sink for Human-Made Carbon Dioxide Measured. 14 March. https://www.sciencedaily. com/releases/2019/03/190314151648.htm.

Sguazzin, A. 2021. World's First Wildlife Bond to Track Rhino Numbers in Africa. *Bloomberg Quint*. 24 March. https://www.bloombergquint.com/business/world-s-first-wildlife-bond-to-track-rhino-populations-in-africa.

Shrikanth, S. 2019. "Green Bond" Market Leaves Wildlife Behind. *Financial Times*. 21 June. https://www.ft.com/content/67d22826-9353-11e9-b7ea-60e35ef678d2.

Spalding, M. J. 2017. The Association of Southeast Asian Nations' Role in Ocean Issues. *The Ocean Foundation*. https://oceanfdn.org/the-association-of-southeast-asian-nations-role-in-ocean-issues/.

Srivastava, S. 2019. What Is a Rhino Bond? Here's All Need to Know. *CNBC*. 18 July. https://www.cnbc.com/2019/07/18/what-is-a-rhino-bond-here-is-all-you-need-to-know.html.

Takehama, S. 1990. In R. S. Shomura and M. L. Godfrey, eds. Estimation of Damage to Fishing Vessels Caused by Marine Debris, Based on Insurance Statistics. Proceedings of the Second International Conference on Marine Debris. Honolulu, Hawaii. 2–7 April 1989. United States Department of Commerce. pp. 792–809. https://repository.library.noaa.gov/view/noaa/6012.

The ASEAN Post. 2017. Southeast Asia's Stream of Polluted Rivers. November. https://theaseanpost.com/article/southeast-asias-stream-polluted-rivers.

The Commonwealth. 2016. Discussion Note Commonwealth. Unlocking Climate Finance for Commonwealth Countries. October. https://thecommonwealth.org/sites/default/files/inline/FMM163%20-%20CFMM_Climate%20Finance.pdf.

The Independent Expert Group on Climate Finance. 2020. *Delivering on the $100 Billion Climate Finance Commitment and Transforming Climate Finance*. December. https://www.un.org/sites/un2.un.org/files/100_billion_climate_finance_report.pdf.

The Nature Conservancy. 2016. Rising Tides: Debt-for-Nature Swaps Let Impact Investors Finance Climate Resilience. 17 June. https://www.nature.org/en-us/what-we-do/our-insights/perspectives/rising-tides-debt-for-nature-swaps-finance-climate-resilience/.

Tierra Resources. Frequently Asked Questions. https://tierraresourcesllc.com/learn-carbon-offsets/frequently-asked-questions/.

Tran, V. 2016. The Most Life-Threatening Issues Facing ASEAN's Oceans. *Cultural Vistas*. 24 February. https://culturalvistas.org/blog/ideas-issues/the-most-life-threatening-issues-facing-asean-oceans/.

Turpie, J.K. et al. 2017. *Promoting Green Urban Development in Africa: Enhancing the Relationship Between Urbanization, Environmental Assets and Ecosystem Services – Msimbazi River Catchment, Dar Es Salaam*. Washington, DC: World Bank. 1 April. https://documents.worldbank.org/en/publication/documents-reports/documentdetail/541771495439323628/enhancing-the-relationship-between-urbanization-environmental-assets-and-ecosystem-services-msimbazi-river-catchment-dar-es-salaam.

United Nations Conference on Trade and Development. Oceans Economy and Fisheries. https://unctad.org/topic/trade-and-environment/oceans-economy.

United Nations Educational, Scientific and Cultural Organization. 2017. Launch of the Ocean and Climate Initiatives Alliance. 24 February. http://www.unesco.org/new/en/media-services/single-view/news/launch_of_the_ocean_and_climate_initiatives_alliance/.

United Nations Environment Programme (UNEP). 2017. *Waste Management in ASEAN Countries: Summary Report*. https://environment.asean.org/wp-content/uploads/2020/03/Summary-Report-Waste-Management-in-ASEAN-Countries-UNEP.pdf.

UNEP. 2018. *Single-use Plastics: A Roadmap for Sustainability*. https://www.unep.org/resources/report/single-use-plastics-roadmap-sustainability.

———. 2019. Agenda Item 5: Consideration of Resolution of UNEP/EA.2/Res.10: Oceans and Seas—Proposal for a New Marine and Coastal Strategy of UN Environment Programme for 2020–2030. 145th Meeting of the Committee of Permanent Representatives to the UNEP. Nairobi. 19 February. https://wedocs.unep.org/bitstream/handle/20.500.11822/27379/5.Proposal for a new Marine and Coastal Strategy of UN Environment Programme for 2020-2030.pdf?sequence=9&isAllowed=y.

———. 2019. UNEP Report Warns Plastic Policies Lagging behind in South-East Asia. 13 November. https://www.unep.org/news-and-stories/press-release/unep-report-warns-plastic-policies-lagging-behind-south-east-asia.

UNEP Finance Initiative. 2021. *Rising Tide: Mapping Ocean Finance for a New Decade*. February. https://www.unepfi.org/publications/rising-tide/.

———. 2021. Turning the Tide: *How to Finance a Sustainable Ocean Recovery: A Practical Guide for Financial Institutions*. March. https://www.unepfi.org/publications/turning-the-tide/.

United Nations Sustainable Development Goals. 2021. Ocean Conference Daily Press Briefing by Damian Cardona Onses (5 June 2017). https://www.un.org/sustainabledevelopment/blog/2017/06/ocean-conference-daily-press-briefing-by-damian-cardona-onses-5-june-2017/.

United States Agency for International Development. 2019. USAID Announces Private-Sector Partnership to Combat Plastic Pollution in the Ocean. 5 June. https://www.usaid.gov/news-information/press-releases/jun-5-2019-usaid-announces-private-sector-partnership-combat-plastic-pollution.

Vanderklift, M. A. et al. 2019. Constraints and Opportunities for Market-Based Finance for the Restoration and Protection of Blue Carbon Ecosystems. *Marine Policy*. 107. September. https://doi.org/10.1016/j.marpol.2019.02.001.

Walsh, M. 2018. *Finance for Pacific Ocean Governance Part 1: Background*. Pacific Ocean Finance Program, Office of the Pacific Ocean Commissioner, and Pacific Island Forum Fisheries Agency. https://sustainability.southpacificislands.travel/wp-content/uploads/2018/10/Finance-for-Pacific-Ocean-Governance-Walsh-2018.pdf.

White, P. 2017. Aquaculture Pollution: An Overview of Issues with a Focus on China, Vietnam, and the Philippines. Washington, DC: World Bank. https://openknowledge.worldbank.org/handle/10986/29249.

World Bank. 2017. Giving Oceans a Break Could Generate US$83 Billion in Additional Benefits for Fisheries. 14 February. https://www.worldbank.org/en/news/press-release/2017/02/14/giving-oceans-a-break-could-generate-83-billion-in-additional-benefits-for-fisheries.

World Bank. 2017. What Is the Blue Economy? 6 June. https://www.worldbank.org/en/news/infographic/2017/06/06/blue-economy.

———. 2018. World Bank Announces New Global Fund for Healthy Oceans. 26 September. https://www.worldbank.org/en/news/press-release/2018/09/26/world-bank-announces-new-global-fund-for-healthy-oceans.

———. 2018. Seychelles Launches World's First Sovereign Blue Bond. 29 October. https://www.worldbank.org/en/news/press-release/2018/10/29/seychelles-launches-worlds-first-sovereign-blue-bond.

———. 2019. World Bank Launched Bonds to Highlight the Challenge of Plastic Waste in Oceans. 3 April. https://www.worldbank.org/en/news/press-release/2019/04/03/world-bank-launches-bonds-to-highlight-the-challenge-of-plastic-waste-in-oceans.

World Economic Forum (WEF). 2019. *From Funding to Financing: Transforming SDG Finance for Country Success*. Geneva. https://www.weforum.org/whitepapers/from-funding-to-financing-transforming-sdg-finance-for-country-success.

WEF. 2020. *Radically Reducing Plastic Pollution in Indonesia: A Multistakeholder Action Plan*. National Plastic Action Partnership. April. https://globalplasticaction.org/wp-content/uploads/NPAP-Indonesia-Multistakeholder-Action-Plan_April-2020.pdf.

World Water Council and OECD. 2015. Water: Fit to Finance? Catalyzing National Growth Through Investment in Water Security. April. https://www.worldwatercouncil.org/en/publications/water-fit-finance.

Willis Towers Watson. Global Ecosystem Resilience Facility. https://www.willistowerswatson.com/en-US/Insights/trending-topics/csp-global-ecosystem-resilience-facility.

WWF. 2019. Pioneering Global Framework for Sustainable Ocean Finance Launched at Our Ocean Global Summit. 29 October. https://wwf.panda.org/wwf_news/press_releases/?337412/Pioneering-global-framework-for-sustainable-ocean-finance-launched-at-Our-Ocean-global-summit.

WWF. Illegal Fishing. https://www.worldwildlife.org/threats/illegal-fishing.

Yonavjak, L. 2016. Environmental Impact Bonds Pay for Performance. *Conservation Finance Network*. 12 January. https://www.conservationfinancenetwork.org/2016/01/12/environmental-impact-bonds-pay-for-performance.